MANUAL FOR
THE PISA 2000 DATABASE

OECD
ORGANISATION FOR ECONOMIC CO-OPERATION AND DEVELOPMENT

ORGANISATION FOR ECONOMIC CO-OPERATION AND DEVELOPMENT

Pursuant to Article 1 of the Convention signed in Paris on 14th December 1960, and which came into force on 30th September 1961, the Organisation for Economic Co-operation and Development (OECD) shall promote policies designed:

– to achieve the highest sustainable economic growth and employment and a rising standard of living in Member countries, while maintaining financial stability, and thus to contribute to the development of the world economy;

– to contribute to sound economic expansion in Member as well as non-member countries in the process of economic development; and

– to contribute to the expansion of world trade on a multilateral, non-discriminatory basis in accordance with international obligations.

The original Member countries of the OECD are Austria, Belgium, Canada, Denmark, France, Germany, Greece, Iceland, Ireland, Italy, Luxembourg, the Netherlands, Norway, Portugal, Spain, Sweden, Switzerland, Turkey, the United Kingdom and the United States. The following countries became Members subsequently through accession at the dates indicated hereafter: Japan (28th April 1964), Finland (28th January 1969), Australia (7th June 1971), New Zealand (29th May 1973), Mexico (18th May 1994), the Czech Republic (21st December 1995), Hungary (7th May 1996), Poland (22nd November 1996), Korea (12th December 1996) and the Slovak Republic (14th December 2000). The Commission of the European Communities takes part in the work of the OECD (Article 13 of the OECD Convention).

TABLE OF CONTENTS

WHAT IS THE GENERAL STRUCTURE OF THE INTERNATIONAL DATABASE?

This document describes the international database of the OECD Programme for International Student Assessment (PISA) 2000. The database comprises data collected in 2000 in 32 countries and processed in the second half of 2000 and in 2001. The first results were released in December 2001 (for the full set of results see OECD, 2001).

The purpose of this document is to provide all of the necessary information to analyse the data in accordance with the methodologies used to collect and process the data. It does not provide detailed information regarding these methods. In addition, a list of related publications can be found in the "Further Reading" section at the end of this document.

The following sources can provide additional information about PISA:

– The **PISA Web page** (_www.pisa.oecd.org_): i) it provides descriptions about the programme, contact information, participating countries and results of PISA 2000, ii) it allows users to download the complete micro-level database, all questionnaires, publications, national reports and the media cover of PISA 2000, and iii) it provides an opportunity for users to generate their own tables or request specific ones.

– The publication **Knowledge and Skills for Life - First Results from PISA 2000** (OECD, 2001) includes the first results from PISA 2000. It presents evidence on student performance in reading, mathematical and scientific literacy, reveals factors that influence the development of these skills at home and at school, and examines what the implications are for policy development.

– The publication **Sample Tasks from the PISA 2000 Assessment - Reading, Mathematical and Scientific Literacy** (OECD, 2002) describes the instruments underlying the PISA assessment. It introduces the PISA approach to assessing reading, mathematical and scientific literacy with its three dimensions of processes, content and context. Further it presents tasks from the PISA 2000 assessment together with how these tasks were scored and how they relate to the conceptual framework underlying PISA.

– The publication **PISA 2000 Technical Report** (OECD, 2002) presents the methodology and procedures used in PISA.

The database provides detailed information on all instruments used in PISA 2000 for the following countries:

– OECD Member Countries: Australia, Austria, Belgium, Canada, the Czech Republic, Denmark, Finland, France, Germany, Greece, Hungary, Iceland, Ireland, Italy, Japan, Korea, Luxembourg, Mexico, the Netherlands, New Zealand, Norway, Poland, Portugal, Spain, Sweden Switzerland, the United Kingdom, and the United States.

– OECD Non-Member Countries: Brazil, Latvia, Liechtenstein, and the Russian Federation.

WHICH INSTRUMENTS WERE INCLUDED IN PISA 2000?

Test design

In PISA 2000, a rotated test design was used to assess student performance in reading, mathematical and scientific literacy (for the complete conceptual frameworks see OECD, 1999b and OECD, 2000). This type of test design ensures a wide coverage of content while at the same time keeping the testing burden on individual students low. Nine test booklets were distributed at random to students. These booklets included questions assessing reading literacy, mathematical literacy and scientific literacy, but not all booklets assessed the same domains. Students were randomly assigned a testing booklet within each of the sampled schools.

- Booklets 8 and 9 contained reading, mathematics and science questions;
- Booklets 1, 3 and 5 contained reading and mathematics questions;
- Booklets 2, 4 and 6 contained reading and science questions; and,
- Booklet 7 contained only reading questions.

As PISA used an age-based sample and sought to be as inclusive as possible, an additional booklet, called *Special Education* (SE, referred to in the database as booklet 0), was developed primarily to assess students who attend special schools, in order to include as many as possible of the 15-year-old students in each country. This special education booklet contained questions assessing the domains of mathematics, reading and science, with a lower difficulty level. This booklet was used in a limited number of countries where the proportion of 15-year-old students in special schools or primary schools was relatively high and it was assigned to all students in these schools.

Questionnaires

Student questionnaires

A student questionnaire was designed to collect information about the student's family, home environment, reading habits, school and everyday activities. This information was later analysed both independently and in relation to performance.

Additionally, the programme included two additional optional questionnaires for students. The first one was a cross curriculum competencies questionnaire asking about students' strategies of self-regulated learning, motivational preferences and self-concept, used in 26 out of the 32 countries. The second one was a computer familiarity questionnaire, including questions about students' use of computers, the availability of computers, and students' self-assessment of their computer skills. This was used in 20 out of the 32 countries.

School questionnaire

The principals or head administrators of the participating schools responded to a school questionnaire covering issues such as the demographics of the school, school staffing, the school environment, human and material educational resources in the school, selection and transfer policies, and educational and decision-making practices in the school.

Structure of the testing session

The student testing session consisted of:

— two 60-minute sessions assessing reading, mathematical and scientific literacy;

— 20-30 minutes for the student questionnaire;

— 10 minutes for the international option of cross curriculum competencies questionnaire; and

— 5 minutes for the international option of computer familiarity questionnaire.

The school principal or head administrator answered a 20-30 minute school questionnaire.

WHAT IS AVAILABLE FROM THE PISA 2000 INTERNATIONAL DATABASE?

What is available for downloading?

The downloadable files are classified into six categories. Some of them are quite small, while others (*e.g.*, the micro-level data files) are quite large, taking a long time to download. The six categories of file are:

Questionnaires

The following questionnaires are available: student questionnaire, cross curriculum competencies questionnaire, computer familiarity questionnaire and school questionnaire. Appendices 1 to 4 of this document show these questionnaires, with the variable name of each item in the left-hand margin. For example:

ST03Q01	Q 3 Are you <female> or <male>?	<Female> <Male> □₁ □₂

Codebooks

The codebooks are useful in relating the actual items from the instruments (assessment tests or questionnaires) to the data available in the data files as they identify the variable name with all possible values which are valid for that variable. In addition to the name of the variable, they also show its label, all possible responses (code and label), type of variable (*e.g.* string or numeric) and the columns where the values are shown in the actual data file. Three codebooks are available: the student questionnaire data file codebook, the school questionnaire codebook, and the student test data codebook. For example, in the case of the previous item (ST03Q01), the codebook shows:

ST03Q01	*Sex – Q3*	F(1.0) 29-29
	1 Female	
	2 Male	
	7 N/A	
	8 M/R	
	9 Mis	

SAS® Control files

These files will read the raw text file, and convert it into a SAS® data file assigning label and values (valid and missing). The five SAS® control files will read and convert: the school questionnaire file, the student questionnaire and reading performance file, the student questionnaire and mathematics performance file, the student questionnaire and science performance file, and finally the assessment file. These files have extension *.SAS.

SPSS® Control files

Similarly to the SAS® control files, these files will read the raw text file, and convert it into a SPSS® data file assigning labels and values (valid and missing). The five SPSS® control files will read and convert: the school questionnaire file, the student questionnaire and reading performance, the student questionnaire and mathematics performance, the student questionnaire and science performance, and finally, the assessment file. The files have extension *.SPS.

Data files in text format

The item by item database is available in text format, which once read by the SAS® or SPSS® control files will be correctly formatted and labelled. As it is, it includes one row for each student with his or her responses to all items. These files have extension *.TXT and are in ASCII form.

Compendia

Compendia show the full item by country results for the three student questionnaires, the school questionnaire and the students' performance. The following files are available: i) student compendium and reading performance, ii) student compendium and mathematics performance, iii) student compendium and science performance, iv) school compendium and reading performance, v) school compendium and mathematics performance, vi) school compendium and science performance, and vii) the test item compendium. There are two types of data for each item: percentages by categories and performance by categories. Standard errors are also reported for the percentages and for the literacy means.

WHICH FILES ARE INCLUDED IN THE PISA 2000 INTERNATIONAL DATABASE?

The PISA international database consists of **five data files**. The files are in text (or ASCII) format and are accompanied by the corresponding SAS® and SPSS® control (syntax) files, which can be used to read the text into a SAS® or SPSS® database. Besides the data collected through the international questionnaire, some countries collected data through national options, which are not included in the international database. These files are quite large as they include one record for each student or school.

How are the files named?

The data files in the international database are named according to the following convention:

□□□ □□□□_□□□□

Five additional characters are used for the three student questionnaire data files.
"_read" for the reading data and their relationship with the student questionnaire data;

"_math" for the mathematics data and their relationship with the student questionnaire data; and,

"_scie" for the science data and their relationship with the student questionnaire data.

The next four characters represent the instruments: "Stud" for the student questionnaire, "Scho" for the school questionnaire and "Cogn" for the tests.

The first three characters of the files are always "Int". This indicates that the file refers to the international data.

The student files

Student and reading performance data files (filename: intstud_read.txt)

For each student who participated in the assessment, the following information is available:

– Identification variables for the country, school and student.

– The student responses on the three questionnaires, *i.e.*, the <u>student questionnaire</u> and the two international options: <u>computer familiarity questionnaire</u> and <u>cross curriculum competencies questionnaire</u>.

– The <u>students' indices</u> derived from the original questions in the questionnaires.

– The students' performance scores in reading.

– The <u>student weights</u> and a country adjustment factor for the reading weights.

– The 80 reading <u>Fay's replicates</u> for the computation of the sampling variance estimates.

Student and mathematics performance data files (filename: intstud_math.txt)

For each student who was assessed with one of the booklets that contain mathematics material, the following information is available:

— Identification variables for the country, school and student.

— The student responses on the three questionnaires, *i.e.*, the <u>student questionnaire</u> and the two international options: <u>computer familiarity questionnaire</u> and <u>cross curriculum competencies questionnaire</u>.

— The <u>students' indices</u> derived from the original questions in the questionnaires.

— The students' performance scores in reading and mathematics.

— The <u>student weights</u> and a country adjustment factor for the mathematics weights.

— The 80 reading <u>Fay's replicates</u> for the computation of the sampling variance estimates.

Student and science performance data files (filename: intstud_scie.txt)

For each student who was assessed with one of the booklets that contain science material, the following information is available:

— Identification variables for the country, school and student.

— The student responses on the three questionnaires, *i.e.*, the <u>student questionnaire</u> and the two international options: <u>computer familiarity questionnaire</u> and <u>cross curriculum competencies questionnaire</u>.

— The <u>students' indices</u> derived from the original questions in the questionnaires.

— The students' performance scores in reading and science.

— The <u>student weights</u> and a country adjustment factor for the science weights.

— The 80 reading <u>Fay's replicates</u> for the computation of the sampling variance estimates.

The school file

The school questionnaire data file (filename: intscho.txt)

For each school that participated in the assessment, the following information is available:

— The identification variables for the country and school.

— The school responses on the <u>school questionnaire</u>.

— The <u>school indices</u> derived from the original questions in the school questionnaire.

— The <u>school weight</u>.

The assessment items data file (filename: intcogn.txt)

For each item included in the test, this file shows the students' responses expressed in a one-digit format. The items from mathematics and science used <u>double-digit coding</u> during marking[1]. A file including these codes was available to national centres.

Which records are included in the international database?

Records included in the database

Student level

– All PISA students who attended one of the two test (assessment) sessions.

– PISA students who only attended the questionnaire session are included if they provided a response to the *father's occupation* questions or the *mother's occupation* questions on the <u>student questionnaire</u> (questions 8 to 11).

School level

– All participating schools — that is, any school where at least 25 per cent of the sampled eligible students were assessed — have a record in the school level international database, regardless of whether the school returned the school questionnaire.

Records excluded from the database

Student level

– Additional data collected by some countries for a national or international option such as a grade sample.

– Sampled students who were reported as not eligible, students who were no longer at school, students who were excluded for physical, mental or linguistic reasons, and students who were absent on the testing day.

– Students who refused to participate in the assessment sessions.

– Students from schools where less than 25 percent of the sampled and eligible students participated.

School level

– Schools where fewer than 25 per cent of the sampled eligible students participated in the testing sessions.

---

1. The responses from open-ended items could give valuable information about students' ideas and thinking, which could be fed back into curriculum planning. For this reason, the marking guides for these items in mathematics and science were designed to include a two-digit marking so that the frequency of various types of correct and incorrect response could be recorded. The first digit was the actual score. The second digit was used to categorise the different kings of response on the basis of the strategies used by the student to answer the item. The international database includes only the first digit.

How are missing data represented?

The coding of the data distinguishes between four different types of missing data:

— *Item level non-response*: 9 for a one-digit variable, 99 for a two-digit variable, 999 for a three-digit variable, and so on. Missing codes are shown in the codebooks. This missing code is used if the student or school principal was expected to answer a question, but no response was actually provided.

— *Multiple or invalid responses*: 8 for a one-digit variable, 98 for a two-digit variable, 998 for a three-digit variable, and so on. This code is used for multiple choice items in both test booklets and questionnaires where an invalid response was provided. This code is not used for open-ended questions.

— *Not applicable*: 7 for a one-digit variable, 97 for a two-digit variables, 997 for a three-digit variable, and so on for the student questionnaire data file and for the school data file. Code "n" is used for a one-digit variable in the test booklet data file. This code is used when it was not possible for the student to answer the question. For instance, this code is used if a question was misprinted or if a question was deleted from the questionnaire by a national centre. The not-applicable codes and code "n" are also used in the test booklet file for questions that were not included in the test booklet that the student received.

— *Not reached items*: all consecutive missing values starting from the end of each test session were replaced by the non-reached code, "r", except for the first value of the missing series, which is coded as missing.

How are students and schools identified?

The student identification from the student files consists of three variables, which together form a unique identifier for each student:

— The country identification variable labelled COUNTRY. The country codes used in PISA are the ISO 3166 country codes.

— The school identification variable labelled SCHOOLID.

— The student identification variable labelled STIDSTD.

A fourth variable has been included to differentiate sub-national entities within countries. This variable (SUBNATIO) is used for four countries as follows:

— *Belgium*. The value "01" is assigned to the French Community and the value "02" is assigned to the Flemish Community.

— *Switzerland*. The value "01" is assigned to the German-speaking community, the value "02" is assigned to the French-speaking community and the value "03" is assigned to the Italian-speaking community.

— *United Kingdom*. The value "01" is assigned to Scotland, the value "02" is assigned to England and the value "03" is assigned to Northern Ireland.

– *Australia*. The eight values "01", "02", "03", "04", "05", "06", "07", "08" are assigned to the Australian Capital Territory, New South Wales, Victoria, Queensland, South Australia, Western Australia, Tasmania and the Northern Territory respectively.

The school identification consists of two variables, which together form a unique identifier for each school:

– The country identification variable labelled COUNTRY. The country codes used in PISA are the ISO 3166 country codes.

– The school identification variable labelled SCHOOLID.

THE WEIGHTS AND REPLICATES

Students included in the final PISA sample for a given country are not equally representative of the full student population. Sampling weights must be applied to compensate for differences in the selection probabilities of students. For example, if students from small schools are oversampled in a country, and survey weights are not applied, the resulting statistics will give too much weight to students in small schools. To account for the sample design during the analyses, so as not to produce biased results, survey weights must be incorporated into the analysis. In general, if students from part of the population (*e.g.*, students in small schools) are oversampled, then the weight associated with those students will reduce the contribution of that group to the overall statistic. If another group (*e.g.*, students in rural areas) are undersampled, then the weight associated with those students will inflate the contribution of that group to the overall statistic. The calculation of these weights can be found in the section "Additional Technical Information".

The reading, mathematics and science weights

In the international data files, the variable called W_FSTUWT is the final student weight (the calculation of student weights is presented later in the document). The sum of the weights constitutes an estimate of the size of the target population, *i.e.*, the number of 15-year old students in that country attending school. In this situation large countries would have a stronger contribution to the results than small countries.

These weights are appropriate for the analysis of data that have been collected from **all assessed students**, such as student questionnaire data, and reading performance data.

Because of the test design, using the reading weights for analysing the mathematics or science data will overweight the students assessed with the SE booklet and therefore (typically) underestimate the results.

To correct this over-weighting of the SE students, weight adjustment factors must be applied to the weights and replicates (see the "Additional Technical Information" section for more detail on the adjustment factors).

Because of the necessity of using these adjustment factors in analyses, and to avoid accidental misuse of the student data, these data are provided in the three separate files described above.

— The file *Instud_read.txt* comprises the reading ability estimates and weights. This file contains all eligible students who participated in the survey. As the sample design assessed reading by all students, no adjustment was needed.

— The file *Instud_math.txt* comprises the reading and mathematics ability estimates. Weights and replicates in this file have already been adjusted by the mathematics adjustment factor. Thus, no further transformations of the weights or replicates are required by analysts of the data.

— The file *Instud_scie.txt* comprises the reading and science ability estimates. Weights and replicates in this file have already been adjusted by the science adjustment factor. Thus, no further transformations of the weights or replicates are required by analysts of the data.

How to analyse the relationship between performance in mathematics and performance in science

As noted in the section on the PISA <u>test design</u>, only two-ninths of students were assessed in both mathematics and science. In order to analyse the relationship between performance in mathematics and science, a separate adjustment factor, NOT provided in the current database, is needed. By the same token, the same adjustment factor is needed to perform any analysis that involves the simultaneous examination of performance in the three domains. Because of the relatively small sample size, an extensive use of this type of analysis must be undertaken with care. However, for users who wish to pursue this type of analysis, the adjustment factor should be: *i)* equal to 0.0 for all students assessed with booklets 1 to 7; *ii)* 4.5 for students assessed with booklets 8 or 9; and *iii)* 1.0 for students assessed with the SE booklet. The final student weight (W_FSTUWT) needs to be multiplied by the adjustment factor associated with each booklet, and the data weighted by the adjusted weight, for analyses which simultaneously include mathematics and science.

Normalising the student weights

If one uses the reading, mathematics and science weights as they are provided in the files and described in the previous section, the total sample size (N) of the output corresponds to an estimate of the number of students in the population in question rather than in the sample.

Population weights can be used without any concerns for most of the statistical analyses. On the other hand, variance decomposition models require that the sum of the weights is equal to the number of observations in the data file, otherwise the estimates of the variance components (i.e. school variance or within school variance) will not be appropriate.

The normalisation of the weights requires that the final weight and the 80 replicates be divided by the sum of the weights for a particular country and then multiplied by the number of observations.

The Fay's replicates

<u>Fay's replicates</u> are included in the data files because they are needed to compute unbiased-standard error estimates associated with any population parameter estimates. The standard error (of sampling) provides an estimate of the degree to which a statistic (such as a mean score) may be expected to vary about the true (but unknown) population mean. A 95% confidence interval for a mean (consisting of a region from 1.96 standard errors below the mean to 1.96 standard errors above the mean) may be constructed in such a way that, if the sampling procedure were repeated a large number of times, and the sample statistic re-computed each time, the confidence interval would be expected to contain the population estimate 95% of the time. Fay's replicates take into account the complex, two-stage, stratified sample design. If this is not done, one underestimates the standard error, thereby running the risk of obtaining statistical significance when in fact there is none. There are several methods of doing this, two of which are described here: a) <u>WesVar®</u>, and b) <u>SAS®</u> or <u>SPSS®</u>.

1. Using WesVar®

Software such as <u>WesVar®</u> (Westat, 2000) estimates sampling variances for complex design through replication methods. This technique involves repeatedly calculating estimates for G subgroups of the sample and then computing the variance among these replicate estimates. The particular method of variance estimation that incorporates the Fay's replicates is known as Fay's Balanced Repeated Replication (BRR) method. BRR is generally used with multistage stratified sample designs, and usually has two units (in this case, schools) in each variance stratum. Using Fay's method, half of the sample is weighted by a factor K (which must be between 0 and 1; for analyses of PISA data, the factor K is set at 0.5), and the other half is weighted by $(2 - K)$.

The three student questionnaires data files contain the 80 replicates that should be used to estimate the sampling variances for the computed statistics. These 80 replicates are called W_FSTR1 to W_FSTR80. The replicates should only be used for analysing the appropriate performance data and for the questionnaire data.

The Fay's replicates included in the mathematics and science files have already been transformed with the adjustment factors mentioned above. Thus the data can be used without additional transformations.

When importing the data into a software package such as WesVar®, the method used to create the replicates has also to be specified. It is of prime importance that the user selects the Fay's method and sets the Fay coefficient (Fay_K) as 0.5. If one does not select the method used for the replicate computation, the software will provide biased estimates of the sampling variance.

2. Using SAS® or SPSS®

The standard errors can also be estimated with more standard statistical packages such as SAS® or SPSS®, as follows:

— Step 1: Calculate each estimate of interest (such as the mean) 81 times — once by weighting the file with the final student weight, and once with each of the replicate weights.

— Step 2: Calculate the sum of the 80 squared differences between each of the replicate estimates in turn and the "full sample" estimate.

— Step 3: Divide the result by 20 to get the variance (The number 20 is correct in the case of PISA as 80 replicates and a Fay coefficient of 0.5 are used. If any of these two components are changed, then 20 is not the correct number anymore).

— Step 4: Take the square root to get the standard error.

Country weight adjustment factors

Each of the three student files contains a country adjustment factor for each assessment domain (CNTRFAC, for reading, CNTMFAC for mathematics, and CNTSFAC for science). These weights will give an equal weight to each country (rather than a weight that reflects the size of the 15-year-old population in that country). In this situation, a small country and a large country would contribute equally to the analysis.

These adjustment factors are designed to set the sum of the student weights for each country to 1,000, so that each country contributes equally in the calculation of a statistic across countries. When analyses are carried out across countries, the country adjustment factors should also be applied to the Fay's replicates.

THE STUDENT QUESTIONNAIRE FILES

The responses to the student questionnaires

The student files contain the original variables collected through the student context questionnaires, *i.e.*, the compulsory <u>student questionnaire</u> and the two international options: the <u>cross-curriculum competencies questionnaire (CCC)</u> and the <u>computer familiarity questionnaire (IT)</u>.

The names that are used to represent these variables in the international database are directly related to the international version of the context questionnaires. Each variable name consists of seven characters.

ST ☐☐ Q ☐☐

The sixth and seventh characters refer to the item number of the question. For instance, ST01Q01 is the day of birth, ST01Q02 is the month of birth and ST01Q03 is the year of birth.

The third and fourth characters refer to the question number as it appears in the international version of the questionnaire. For instance, ST01 refers to the first question in the student questionnaire relating to the date of birth.

The first two characters refer to the instrument:
ST for the student questionnaire,
IT for the computer familiarity questionnaire,
CC for the cross curriculum competencies questionnaire.

The student performance scores

Performance scores

For each domain, *i.e.*, reading, mathematics and science, and for each subscale in reading, two kinds of estimate are provided: a <u>weighted likelihood estimate (WLE)</u> and a set of <u>plausible values</u>.

It is recommended that the set of plausible values be used when analysing and reporting statistics at the population level. Using WLEs for population estimates will yield biased estimates.

The weighted likelihood estimates

The international database provides six weighted likelihood estimates and their standard errors, respectively labelled:

- variable WLEREAD to represent the reading ability estimate, which is provided for all students who answered at least one reading question;

- variable WLEREAD1 to represent the reading ability estimate for the retrieving subscale, which is provided for all students who answered at least one reading retrieving question;

- variable WLEREAD2 to represent the reading ability estimate for the interpreting subscale, which is provided for all students who answered at least one reading interpreting question;

- variable WLEREAD3 to represent the reading ability estimate for the reflecting and evaluating subscale, which is provided for all students who answered at least one reading reflecting and evaluating question;

- variable WLEMATH to represent the mathematics ability estimate, which is provided only for students who took booklets 1, 3, 5, 8, 9 or the special booklet and answered at least one mathematics question; and

- variable WLESCIE to represent the science ability estimate, which is provided only for students who took booklets 2, 4, 6, 8, 9 or the special booklet and answered at least one science question.

The plausible values

The plausible values represent a set of random values for each selected student at random from an estimated ability distribution of students with similar item response patterns and backgrounds. They are intended to provide good estimates of parameters of student populations (for example, country mean scores), rather than estimates of individual student proficiency, which are better estimated using the weighted likelihood estimates.

The international database provides five plausible values for each domain and each reading subscale, respectively labelled:

- PV1read to PV5read for reading ability,

- PV1read1 to PV5read1 for reading ability, *retrieving information* subscale,

- PV1read2 to PV5read2 for reading ability, *interpreting* subscale,

- PV1read3 to PV5read3 for reading ability, *reflecting and evaluating* subscale,

- PV1math to PV5math for mathematics ability,

- PV1scie to PV5scie for science ability.

Each student included in the international database has performance plausible values for the reading domain as well as for the reading subscales. Only students who were assessed with booklets 1, 3, 5, 8, 9 and the special booklet, will have plausible values in mathematics, and only students who were assessed with booklets 2, 4, 6, 8, 9 and the special booklet will have plausible values in science.

Transformation of the ability estimates

The weighted likelihood estimates and the plausible values were transformed to a scale with a mean of 500 and a standard deviation of 100 by using the data for the participating OECD countries only (except the Netherlands [2]). These linear transformations used weighted data, with an additional adjustment factor so that each country contributed equally. The standardisation parameters were derived from the average of the mean and standard deviation computed from each of the five plausible values. This means that although the mean and standard deviation of individual plausible values will not be exactly 500 and 100, respectively, the average of the five means and the five standard deviations for each scale will be 500 and 100, respectively.

The transformation that was used to give reading a mean of 500 and a standard deviation of 100 was also applied to the three reading subscales. This means that the mean and the standard deviation for the reading subscales will differ from 500 and 100, respectively.

---

2. Response rate too low to ensure comparability (Annex A3, OECD (2001)).

To retrieve the mean of 500 and the standard deviation of 100, the following steps should be followed during data analysis:

1. Delete the data from the non-OECD countries (Brazil, Latvia, Liechtenstein and Russia) and from the Netherlands.

2. Transform the final weight (and the 80 Fay's replicates in the computation of the standard error is required) to equalise the contribution of each remaining countries. This transformation can be implemented by multiplying the final weight and 80 replicates by the appropriate country adjustment factor mentioned above.

3. For each plausible value, compute the mean and the standard deviation

4. Average the five mean estimates and the five standard deviation estimate.

Figure 1 presents the SAS® syntax for step 1 to 3 mentioned above.

Figure 1

SAS® syntax for calculating the mean of 500 and the standard deviation of 100

```
data pisa.tempo;
set pisa.studread;
if (cnt="NLD") then delete;
if (cnt="LVA") then delete;
if (cnt="LIE") then delete;
if (cnt="RUS") then delete;
if (cnt="BRA") then delete;
array poids(81)
w_fstuwt w_fstr1-w_fstr80;
do i=1 to 81;
    poids(i)=(poids(i)* cntrfac);
end;
run;
proc means data=pisa.tempo vardef=wgt;
var pv1read pv2read pv3read pv4read pv5read;
weight w_fstuwt;
run;
```

How to analyse data using the plausible values

It is important to recognise that plausible values are not test scores and should not be treated as such. As noted above, plausible values are random numbers that are drawn from the distribution of scores that could be reasonably assigned to each individual. As such, the plausible values contain random error variance components (that is, variation between individual plausible values assigned to each student) and are not optimal as scores for individuals. However, the important characteristic of plausible values is that as a set, they are better suited for describing the performance of the population than a set of scores that are optimal at the individual student level (for example, the weighted likelihood estimates).

Plausible values can be thought of as intermediate values that provide consistent estimates of population parameters. Such estimates can be obtained using statistical software such as WesVar®, SPSS® and SAS®.

During data exploration, there is no need to work with the five plausible values; one can use a single plausible value. On average, one plausible value will provided unbiased estimates of population parameters. However for the final estimates, it is recommended that all five plausible values be used, otherwise the standard error estimated from one plausible value will only contain the sampling variance component while it should also contain the measurement error component. This means that the analysis should be undertaken five times, once with each of the five relevant plausible values. The results of these five analyses need to be combined so that the associated standard error incorporates measurement error associated with the variance between the five plausible values. The method for combining them is described below in two sections: one for users of the WesVar® software, and one for users of the SAS® and SPSS® software systems. An example of computing correlation using plausible values is included later in the document.

1. Using WesVar®

The WesVar® software can incorporate the five plausible values and produce the correct standard errors in the calculation of means of groups, using the 'PV' function. The degrees of freedom that WesVar® uses for these analyses are not the actual degrees of freedom but rather the number of replicate weights, 80 in the case of the PISA database. This is considered an accurate approximation to the actual degrees of freedom for the vast majority of analyses.

For other types of estimate, such as quartiles or medians, the analysis in question must be carried out five times and the five estimates combined as described in the section on SAS® and SPSS® that follows.

2. Using SAS® and SPSS®

As computer packages such as SAS® and SPSS® do not provide standard (measurement) errors associated with estimates, it is necessary to compute such standard errors using the following procedure. (Note that WesVar® only provides correct standard errors associated with means, so all other types of analysis done in WesVar® should also be undertaken using the procedures below.)

1. Separate estimates need to be computed for each plausible value. This will result in five estimated parameters (one associated with each plausible value). Each set (P1 to P5) should then be averaged to provide a mean parameter estimate (MP). Standard errors (SE1 to SE5) also need to be generated for each parameter estimate (P1 to P5).

2. The measurement error and sampling variances for the mean parameter estimate (MP) should then be computed. The measurement error variance should be computed using the following formula:

$$[(MP\text{-}P1)^2 + (MP\text{-}P2)^2 + (MP\text{-}P3)^2 + (MP\text{-}P4)^2 + (MP\text{-}P5)^2]/4$$

The sampling variance should be computed using the following formula:

$$[(SE1^2 + SE2^2 + SE3^2 + SE4^2 + SE5^2)]/5$$

The total variance should then be computed by summing the measurement error and the sampling variances. In doing so, a weight of 1.2 (1 + 1/M, where M is the number of plausible values) should be applied to the measurement error variance. The square root of the total variance provides an estimate of the standard error of the parameter estimate. Note that outputs from SAS®, SPSS® and WesVar® can be pasted into spreadsheet packages such as Excel, which can then be used to semi-automate this procedure, if many such analyses are to be undertaken. An example of how an Excel spreadsheet can be set up is given in Figure 2, below.[3]

Figure 2

Formulae for computation of standard errors of plausible values in Excel

Plausible Value	Parameter Estimate	Standard Error*
1	[a1]	[b1]
2	[a2]	[b2]
3	[a3]	[b3]
4	[a4]	[b4]
5	[a5]	[b5]

Sampling variance	=(b1^2+b2^2+b3^2+b4^2+b5^2)/5 **[a6]**
Mean parameter estimate	=(a1+a2+a3+a4+a5)/5 **[a7]**
Measurement variance	=((a1-a7)^2+(a2-a7)^2+(a3-a7)^2+(a4-a7)^2+(a5-a7)^2)/4 **[a8]**
Variance of parameter estimate	=a6+(1.2*a8) **[a9]**
Corrected standard error	*=sqrt(a9)*

* If SAS® or SPSS® are used, then the SE should be estimated as previously described

How to analyse the data using the proficiency scale levels

PISA 2000 assessed reading literacy as the major domain, while keeping mathematics and science as minor domains. That means that two-thirds of the assessment was in reading literacy tasks. The reading scales were divided into five levels of knowledge and skills, facilitating their interpretation, and because of the manner in which the PISA performance data have been scaled, it is possible to describe what students scoring at around a particular point are able to do. Because both item difficulties and student performance scores are scaled to the same metric, one can examine items of similar difficulty and make inferences about the underlying skills and complexity of reasoning that are required to respond correctly to such clusters of items. Therefore, the application of techniques associated with item response theory to the PISA performance data means that it is possible to generate a criterion-referenced interpretation of student proficiency. The creation of proficiency levels is extremely useful from a policy and pedagogical point of view because it provides a shorthand description of what students in each group are likely to be able to do. Comparisons of the proportions of students at each proficiency level within and between

---

3. Formulae kindly provided by Keith Rust and Sheila Krawchuk of Westat, Inc.

countries can yield useful information about the relative strengths and weaknesses of groups of students. The development of the proficiency levels for PISA involved establishing appropriate cut-off points for each level, and developing a substantive description of the skills and knowledge associated with each level through a detailed examination of the items associated with these levels. The process of developing proficiency levels is thus an iterative one. Subject-matter experts and technical experts of the PISA consortium worked together to produce them.

PISA proficiency levels were defined in such a way that a student with a reading score at the bottom of a level has an average probability of .50 of correctly responding to all items at that level. Application of this criterion, and a further criterion that proficiency levels should be of fixed width (.80 logits), led to the establishment of a response probability convention of .62[4]. The label 'below Level 1' is assigned to students who did not meet the criterion for Level 1 (*i.e.*, the estimated probability of these students responding correctly to items at the bottom of Level 1 is less than .50). PISA does not describe what students below Level 1 can accomplish[5]. Similarly, PISA does not describe the upper limits of the knowledge and skills of students at Level 5 on the scales (*i.e.*, students at this level may have additional skills not assessed by PISA).

The cut-off points for the reading scales and its three subscales are 334.75, 407.47, 480.18, 552.89 and 625.61. The five levels are defined in Figure 3.

Figure 3

Cut points for proficiency levels for the PISA combined literacy scale and the three literacy subscales

---

Level 0: the reading score is equal to or below 334.75;

Level 1: the reading score is greater than 334.75 and equal to or below 407.47;

Level 2: the reading score is greater than 407.47 and equal to or below 480.18;

Level 3: the reading score is greater than 480.18 and equal to or below 552.89;

Level 4: the reading score is greater than 552.89 and equal to or below 625.61;

Level 5: the reading score is greater than 625.61.

---

4. For analysts familiar with the International Adult Literary Survey (IALS), it is pertinent to point out that the response probability associated with the IALS proficiency levels was set at .80. This more stringent criterion means, in effect, that one must be more certain that a person can correctly respond to items associated with a particular proficiency level in order categorise that individual as belonging to that level. This is especially relevant if analysts of the PISA 2000 international database are making comparisons between performance on the PISA assessment of reading literacy and performance on IALS.

5. Referring again to the IALS study, no distinction was made between students whose scores were below level 1. This may also be relevant to those wishing to make comparisons between the two studies.

To estimate the percentages of students in each of the six levels, five new categorical variables should be computed, one for each of the five plausible values provided by each scale or subscale, using the type of syntax shown in Figure 4, taken from SPSS®. It is acceptable to combine levels, such as Level 1 and below Level 1, but advisable that explicit note of this is made to prevent misinterpretation of results.

Figure 4

SPSS® syntax used to create six proficiency levels for each plausible value

---

*individual plausible values: proficiency levels for overall reading produces a proficiency

*level pvp1, pvp2, etc. associated with each plausible value, pv1read, pv2read, etc.

IF (pv1read le 334.75) pvp1 = 0.

IF (pv1read gt 334.75) pvp1 = 1.

IF (pv1read gt 407.47) pvp1 = 2.

IF (pv1read gt 480.18) pvp1 = 3.

IF (pv1read gt 552.89) pvp1 = 4.

IF (pv1read gt 625.61) pvp1 = 5.

IF (pv2read le 334.75) pvp2 = 0.

IF (pv2read gt 334.75) pvp2 = 1.

IF (pv2read gt 407.47) pvp2 = 2.

IF (pv2read gt 480.18) pvp2 = 3.

IF (pv2read gt 552.89) pvp2 = 4.

IF (pv2read gt 625.61) pvp2 = 5.

(… and so on for each of the five plausible values.)

Percentages and sampling variance can be estimated with WesVar® for each of these categorical variables. The results then need to be combined as described above (see Figure 1).

It is possible to shortcut this procedure by generating for each plausible value six dichotomous variables coded 0,1 (below level 1 or not, at level 1 or not, at level 2 or not, …. at level 5 or not). Therefore, 30 dichotomous variables need to be computed. As the percentage of students for these dichotomous variables can be estimated by computing the mean, then it becomes possible to use the *PV function* in WesVar®. The standard error will therefore consists of the sampling variance and the measurement error. Figure 5 shows the SAS syntax to generate the 30 dichotomous variables.

SAS® syntax to generate the proficiency levels using 30 dichotomous variables

```
array reading (5)
    pv1read pv2read pv3read pv4read pv5read;
array level0 (5)
            lev1r1-lev1r5;
array level1 (5)
            lev2r1-lev2r5;
array level2 (5)
            lev3r1-lev3r5;
array level3 (5)
            lev4r1-lev4r5;
array level4 (5)
            lev5r1-lev5r5;
array level5 (5)
            lev6r1-lev6r5;
do i=1 to 5;
level0(i)=0;
level1(i)=0;
level2(i)=0;
level3(i)=0;
level4(i)=0;
level5(i)=0;
if (reading(i)<=334.75) then level0(i)=1;
if (reading(i)> 334.75 and reading(i)<= 407.47) then level1(i)=1;
if (reading(i)>407.47 and reading(i)<=480.18) then level2(i)=1;
if (reading(i)>480.18 and reading (i)<=552.89) then level3(i)=1;
if (reading(i)>552.89 and reading (i)<=625.61) then level4(i)=1;
if (reading(i)>625.61) then level5(i)=1;
end;
```

Once these 30 variables are imported into WesVar®, then the *PV function* can be used and results do not need to be imported in an Excel® spreadsheet to be combined.

The student questionnaire indices

Several of PISA's measures reflect indices that summarise responses from students or school representatives (typically principals) to a series of related questions. The questions were selected from larger constructs on the basis of theoretical considerations and previous research. Structural equation modelling was used to confirm the theoretically expected behaviour of the indices and to validate their comparability across countries. For this purpose, a model was estimated separately for each country and, collectively, for all OECD countries.

This section explains the indices derived from the student and school context questionnaires that are used in this report. For a description of other PISA indices and details on the methods see the *PISA 2000 Technical Report*.

Unless otherwise indicated, where an index involves multiple questions and student responses, the index was scaled using a weighted maximum likelihood estimate, using a one-parameter item response model (referred to as a WARM estimator; see Warm, 1985) with three stages:

- The question parameters were estimated from equal-sized sub-samples of students from each OECD country.
- The estimates were computed for all students and all schools by anchoring the question parameters obtained in the preceding step.
- The indices were then standardised so that the mean of the index value for the OECD student population was zero and the standard deviation was one (countries being given equal weight in the standardisation process).

It is important to note that negative values in an index do not necessarily imply that students responded negatively to the underlying questions. A negative value merely indicates that a group of students (or all students, collectively, in a single country) or principals responded less positively than all students or principals did on average across OECD countries. Likewise, a positive value on an index indicates that a group of students or principals responded more favourably, or more positively, than students or principals did, on average, in OECD countries.

Terms enclosed in brackets < > in the following descriptions were replaced in the national versions of the student and school questionnaires by the appropriate national equivalent. For example, the term <qualification at ISCED level 5A> was translated in the United States into "Bachelor's Degree, post-graduate certificate program, Master's degree program or first professional degree program". Similarly the term <classes in the language of assessment> in Luxembourg was translated into "German classes" or "French classes" depending on whether students received the German or French version of the assessment instruments.

For the reliabilities of the indices, see the *PISA 2000 Technical Report*.

Indices derived through a direct combination of the answers from the student questionnaire

The following indices were included in the student questionnaire file:

- *Time in minutes spent each week at school in reading (RMINS), mathematics (MMINS) and science (SMINS) courses.* The three variables are simply the product of the following corresponding items:

    • How many <class periods> the students spent in courses in each of the three domains during the last full week (ST27Q01 for <test language> courses, ST27Q03 for <mathematics> courses, and ST27Q05 for <science> courses); and

- The number of instructional minutes in the average single <class period> from the school questionnaire (SC06Q03).

– **Age (AGE)**. The age of the student expressed in months computed from the students' date of birth (ST01).

– **Family structure (FAMSTRUC)**. Students were asked to report who usually lived at home with them. The responses were then grouped into four categories:

- *single-parent family* – coded as 1 (students who reported living with one of the following: mother, father, female guardian or male guardian);

- *nuclear family* – coded as 2 (students who reported living with a mother and a father);

- *mixed family* – coded as 3 (students who reported living with a mother and a male guardian, a father and a female guardian, or two guardians); and

- *other response combinations* – coded as 4.

– **Number of siblings (NSIB)**. Students were asked to indicate how many brothers and sisters they had older than themselves, younger than themselves, or of the same age. For the analyses in Chapter 8 (OECD, 2001), the numbers in each category were added together. This variable is based on the three items of question ST05.

– **Birth order (BRTHORD)**. Also based on ST05, this received a value of 0 if the student was the only child, 1 if the student was the youngest child, 2 if the student was a middle child, and 3 if the student was the oldest child.

– **Father's occupation (BFMJ), mother's occupation (BMMJ) and student's expected occupation at the age of 30 (BTHR)**. Students were asked to report their mothers' and fathers' occupations, and to state whether each parent was: in full-time paid work; part-time paid work; not working but looking for a paid job; or "other". The students' open-ended responses to questions ST08Q01, ST09Q01, ST10Q01 ST11Q01 and ST40Q01 were then coded in accordance with the International Standard Classification of Occupations (ISCO 1988), with these variables receiving the actual ISCO code and later recoded according to the *PISA International Socio-Economic Index of Occupational Status* (ISEI) explained below.

– **PISA International Socio-Economic Index of Occupational Status (ISEI)**. Additionally, these variables were transformed to create the PISA International Socio-Economic Index of Occupational Status, derived from students' responses on parental occupation. The index captures the attributes of occupations that convert parents' education into income. The index was derived by the optimal scaling of occupation groups to maximise the indirect effect of education on income through occupation and to minimise the direct effect of education on income, net of occupation (both effects being net of age). For more information on the methodology, see Ganzeboom *et al.* (1992). The ISEI variable is equal to the father's occupation or to the mother's occupation if the father's ISEI is missing. A second variable is also included (HISEI), based on either the father's or mother's occupations, whichever is the higher. Values on the index range from 16 to 90; low values represent low socio-economic status and high values represent high socio-economic status.

— *Parental education (FISCED for fathers and MISCED for mothers)*. Students were asked to classify the highest level of education of their mother and father on the basis of national qualifications, which were then coded in accordance with the International Standard Classification of Education (ISCED 1997) in order to obtain internationally comparable categories of educational attainment. These were collected in two questions about each parent (questions ST12Q01 and ST14Q01 for the mother and questions ST13Q01 and ST15Q01 for the father). The father's educational level (FISCED) and the mother's educational level (MISCED) have the following categories, which are defined in accordance with the International Student Classification of Education (ISCED) (OECD, 1999*a*):

1. Did not go to school;

2. Completed <ISCED Level 1 only (primary education)>;

3. Completed <ISCED Level 2 only (lower secondary level)>;

4. Completed <ISCED Level 3B or 3C only (upper secondary level, aimed in most countries at providing direct entry into the labour market)>;

5. Completed <ISCED Level 3A (upper secondary, aimed in most countries at gaining entry into tertiary education)>; and

6. Completed <ISCED Level 5A, 5B or 6 (tertiary education)>.

Note: *Years of schooling* was used in Chapter 8 of the First Results from PISA 2000 (OECD, 2001) as a conversion of the highest level of educational attainment of the parents.

Weighted likelihood estimate indices

Indices from the student questionnaire

Fifteen indices from the student questionnaire were derived using the weighted estimate method (Warm, 1985). These indices are:

— *Index of cultural communication with parents (CULTCOM)*. This index was derived from students' reports on the frequency with which their parents (or guardians) engaged with them in the following activities: discussing political or social issues; discussing books, films or television programmes; and listening to classical music. It was based on questions ST19Q01, ST19Q02 and ST19Q03.

— *Index of social communication with parents (SOCCOM)*. This index was derived from students' reports on the frequency with which their parents (or guardians) engaged with them in the following activities: discussing how well they are doing at school; eating <the main meal> with them around a table; and spending time simply talking with them. It was based on questions ST19Q04, ST19Q05 and ST19Q06.

— *Index of family educational support (FAMEDSUP)*. This index was derived from the students' reports on the frequency with which the following people work with them on their schoolwork: their mother, their father, their brothers and sisters. It was derived from questions ST20Q01, ST20Q02 and ST20Q03.

– *Index of family wealth (WEALTH)*. This index was derived from students' reports on: *i)* the availability, in their home, of a dishwasher, a room of their own, educational software, and a link to the Internet; and *ii)* the number of cellular phones, television sets, computers, motor cars and bathrooms at home. It was based on questions ST21Q01, ST21Q02, ST21Q03, ST21Q04, ST22Q01, ST22Q02, ST22Q04, ST22Q06 AND ST22Q07.

– *Index of home educational resources (HEDRES)*. This index was derived from students' reports on: *i)* the availability, in their home, of a dictionary, a quiet place to study, a desk for study, and textbooks; and *ii)* the number of calculators at home. It was based on questions ST21Q05, ST21Q06, ST21Q07, ST21Q08, ST22Q03.

– *Index of activities related to "classical" culture (CULTACTV)*. This index was derived from students' reports on how often they had participated in the following activities during the preceding year: visited a museum or art gallery; attended an opera, ballet or classical symphony concert; and watched live theatre. It was derived from questions ST18Q02, ST18Q04 and ST18Q05.

– *Index of possessions related to "classical" culture in the family home (CULTPOSS)*. This index was derived from students' reports on the availability of the following items in their home: classical literature (examples were given); and books of poetry and works of art (examples were given). It was based on questions ST21Q09, ST21Q10 and ST21Q11.

– *Index of time spent on homework (HMWKTIME)*. This index was derived from students' reports on the amount of time they devote to homework per week in the <language of assessment>, mathematics, and science. It was based on questions ST33Q01, ST33Q02 and ST33Q03.

– *Index of teacher support (TEACHSUP)*. This index was derived from students' reports on the frequency with which: the teacher shows an interest in every student's learning; the teacher gives students an opportunity to express opinions; the teacher helps students with their work; the teacher continues teaching until the students understand; the teacher does a lot to help students; and, the teacher helps students with their learning. It was derived from questions ST26Q05, ST26Q06, ST26Q07, ST26Q08, ST26Q09 and ST26Q10.

– *Index of disciplinary climate (DISCLIMA)*. This index derived from students' reports on the frequency with which, in their <language of assessment class>: the teacher has to wait a long time for students to <quieten down>; students cannot work well; students don't listen to what the teacher says; students don't start working for a long time after the lesson begins; there is noise and disorder; and, at the start of class, more than five minutes are spent doing nothing. It was based on questions ST26Q01, ST26Q12, ST26Q13, ST26Q14, ST26Q16 and ST26Q17. This index was inverted during reporting so that low values indicate a poor disciplinary climate (OECD, 2001).

– *Index of teacher-student relations (STUDREL)*. This index was derived from students' reports on their level of agreement with the following statements: students get along well with most teachers; most teachers are interested in students' well-being; most of their teachers really listen to what they have to say; if they need extra help, they will receive it from their teachers; and, most of their teachers treat them fairly. It was based on questions ST30Q01 to ST30Q05.

— *Index of achievement press (ACHPRESS)*. This index was derived from students' reports on the frequency with which, in their <language of assessment class>: the teacher wants students to work hard; the teacher tells students that they can do better; the teacher does not like it when students deliver <careless> work; and, students have to learn a lot. It was based on questions ST26Q02, ST26Q03, ST26Q04 and ST26Q15.

— *Index of student's sense of belonging in the school (BELONG)*. This index was derived from students' reports on their level of agreement with the following statements concerning their school: I feel like an outsider (or left out of things); I make friends easily; I feel like I belong; I feel awkward and out of place; other students seem to like me; and, I feel lonely. It was based on questions ST31Q01 to ST31Q06.

— *Index of engagement in reading (JOYREAD)*. This index was derived from students' level of agreement with the following statements: I read only if I have to; reading is one of my favourite hobbies; I like talking about books with other people; I find it hard to finish books; I feel happy if I receive a book as a present; for me, reading is a waste of time; I enjoy going to a bookstore or a library; I read only to get information that I need; and, I cannot sit still and read for more than a few minutes. It was based on questions ST35Q01 to ST35Q09.

— *Index of reading diversity (DIVREAD)*. This index was derived from the frequency with which students read the following materials because they wanted to: magazines, comic books, fiction (examples were given), non-fiction books, emails and Web pages, and newspapers. It was based on questions ST36Q01 to ST36Q06. For this index, categories 1 and 2 were recoded as 0 and categories 3, 4, 5 were recoded as 1.

These indices, based on weighted estimates (Warm, 1985), were standardised to have a mean of 0 and a standard deviation of 1 at the international level using the same procedures that were applied to the performance variables. Suggestions for ways of analysing these indices are given in the sub-section on "Analysis of the questionnaire data".

The indices from the cross curricular competencies questionnaire

Fourteen indices from the student cross-curriculum competencies questionnaire (also known as CCC questionnaire) were derived using the weighted estimate method (Warm, 1985). These indices are:

— *Index of control strategies (CSTRAT)*. This index was derived from the frequency with which students used the following strategies when studying: I start by figuring out what exactly I need to learn; I force myself to check to see if I remember what I have learned; I try to figure out, as I read, which concepts I still haven't really understood; I make sure that I remember the most important things; and, when I study and I don't understand something, I look for additional information to clarify the point. It was based on questions CC01Q03, CC01Q13, CC01Q19, CC01Q23 and CC01Q27. For information on the conceptual underpinning of the index see Baumert *et al.* (1994).

— *Index of effort and perseverance (EFFPER)*. This index was derived from the frequency with which students used the following strategies when studying: I work as hard as possible; I keep working even if the material is difficult; I try to do my best to acquire the knowledge and skills taught; and, I put forth my best effort. It was based on questions CC01Q07, CC01Q12, CC01Q20 and CC01Q28.

– *Index of memorisation strategies (MEMOR)*. This index was derived from the frequency with which students used the following strategies when studying: I try to memorise everything that might be covered; I memorise as much as possible; I memorise all new material so that I can recite it; and, I practise by saying the material to myself over and over. It was based on questions CC01Q01, CC01Q05, CC01Q10 and CC01Q15. For information on the conceptual underpinning of the index see Baumert *et al*. (1994) and Pintrich *et al*. (1993).

– *Index of perceived self-efficacy (SELFEF)*. This index was derived from the frequency with which students used the following strategies when studying: I am certain I can understand the most difficult material presented in readings; I am confident I can do an excellent job on assignments and tests; and, I am certain I can master the skills being taught. It was based on questions CC01Q02, CC01Q18 and CC01Q26.

– *Index of control expectations (CEXP)*. This index was derived from the frequency with which students used the following strategies when studying: when I sit myself down to learn something really hard, I can learn it; if I decide not to get any bad grades, I can really do it; if I decide not to get any problems wrong, I can really do it; and, if I want to learn something well, I can. It was based on questions CC01Q04, CC01Q11, CC01Q16 and CC01Q24.

– *Index of elaboration strategies (ELAB)*. This index was derived from the frequency with which students used the following strategies when studying: I try to relate new material to things I have learned in other subjects; I figure out how the information might be useful in the real world; I try to understand the material better by relating it to things I already know; and, I figure out how the material fits in with what I have learned. It was based on questions CC01Q09, CC01Q17, CC01Q21 and CC01Q25. For information on the conceptual underpinning of the index see Baumert *et al*. (1994).

– *Index of instrumental motivation (INSMOT)*. This index was derived from the frequency with which students study for the following reasons: to increase my job opportunities; to ensure that my future will be financially secure; and, to get a good job. It was based on questions CC01Q06, CC01Q14 and CC01Q22.

– *Index of interest in mathematics (INTMAT)*. This index was derived from students' level of agreement with the following statements: when I do mathematics, I sometimes get totally absorbed; mathematics is important to me personally; and, because doing mathematics is fun, I wouldn't want to give it up. It was based on questions CC02Q01, CC02Q10 and CC02Q21. For information on the conceptual underpinning of the index see Baumert *et al*. (1997).

– *Index of self-concept in mathematics (MATCON)*. This index was derived from students' level of agreement with the following statements: I get good marks in mathematics; mathematics is one of my best subjects; and, I have always done well in mathematics. It was based on questions CC02Q12, CC02Q15 and CC02Q18. For information on the conceptual underpinning of the index see Marsh *et al*. (1992).

- *Index of interest in reading (INTREA)*. This index was derived from students' level of agreement with the following statements: because reading is fun, I wouldn't want to give it up; I read in my spare time; and, when I read, I sometimes get totally absorbed. It was based on questions CC02Q06, CC02Q13 and CC02Q17. For information on the conceptual underpinning of the index see Baumert *et al*. (1997).

- *Index of self-concept academics (SCACAD)*. This index was derived from students' level of agreement with the following statements: I learn things quickly in most school subjects; I am good at most school subjects; and I do well in tests in most school subjects. It was based on questions CC02Q03, CC02Q07 and CC02Q20.

- *Index of self-concept in reading (SCVERB)*. This index was derived from students' level of agreement with the following statements: I'm hopeless in <language of assessment classes>; I learn things quickly in the <language of assessment classes>; and, I get good marks in the <language of assessment>. It is based on questions CC02Q05, CC02Q09 and CC02Q23. For information on the conceptual underpinning of the index see Marsh *et al*. (1992).

- *Index of competitive learning (COMLRN)*. This index was derived from students' level of agreement with the following statements: I like to try to be better than other students; trying to be better than others makes me work well; I would like to be the best at something; and, I learn things faster if I'm trying to do better than the others. It is based on questions CC02Q04, CC02Q11, CC02Q16 and CC02Q24. For information on the conceptual underpinning of the index see Owens and Barnes (1992).

- *Index of co-operative learning (COPLRN)*. This index was derived from students' level of agreement with the following statements: I like to work with other students; I learn the most when I work with other students; I like to help other people do well in a group; and, it is helpful to put together everyone's ideas when working on a project. It is based on questions CC02Q02, CC02Q08, CC02Q19 and CC02Q22. For information on the conceptual underpinning of the index see Owens and Barnes (1992).

These indices, based on weighted estimates (Warm, 1985), were standardised to have a mean of 0 and a standard deviation of 1 at the international level using the same procedures as were applied to the performance variables. Only OECD countries (except Netherlands) that participated in the international cross-curriculum competencies option (CCC questionnaire) were included in this transformation.[6]

Indices from the computer familiarity questionnaire

Three indices from the student computer familiarity questionnaire were derived using the weighted estimate method (Warm, 1985). These indices are:

- *Index of comfort with and perceived ability to use computers (COMAB)*. This index was derived from students' responses to the following questions: how comfortable are you with using a computer?; how comfortable are you with using a computer to write a paper?; how comfortable are you with

---

6. Note that Scotland participated while England and Northern Ireland did not. Therefore, Scotland was not included in the countries that contribute to the standardisation.

taking a test on a computer?; and, if you compare yourself with other 15-year-olds, how would you rate your ability to use a computer? It was based on questions IT02Q01, IT02Q02, IT02Q03, and IT03Q01. The items were inverted. For information on the conceptual underpinning of the index see Eignor *et al.* (1998).

– **Index of computer usage (COMUSE)**. This index was derived from students' responses to the frequency to which they use the computer for the following purposes: to help them learn school material; for programming; for word processing (examples of software packages were given); spreadsheets (examples of software packages were given); drawing, painting or graphics; and, educational software. It was based on questions IT05Q03, IT05Q04, IT06Q02, IT06Q03, IT06Q04, and IT06Q05. The items were inverted.

– **Index of interest in computers (COMATT)**. This index was derived from students' responses to the following statements: it is very important to me to work with a computer; to play or work with a computer is really fun; I use a computer because I am very interested in this; and, I forget the time, when I am working with the computer. It is based on questions IT07Q01, IT08Q01, IT09Q01, and IT10Q01. The items were inverted. For information on the conceptual underpinning of the index see Eignor *et al.* (1998).

These indices, based on weighted estimates (Warm, 1985), were standardised to have a mean of 0 and a standard deviation of 1 at the international level using the same procedures as were applied to the performance variables. Only OECD countries (except Netherlands) that participated in the optional computer familiarity component (IT questionnaire) were included in this transformation.

Analysis of the questionnaire data

This section presents a suggestion for analysing the questionnaire data through the aggregation of variables.

Aggregating variables

Some variables from the student questionnaire can be aggregated to the school level for specific analysis since they represent measures of school climate or provide a proxy for the socio-economic status of the student body. Aggregation can be especially useful if one is carrying out multilevel analyses of performance. The amount of between-school variation with respect to these variables may also be of interest in and of itself (*i.e.*, outside student performance); for example, the between-school variability associated with the International Socio-Economic Index of Occupational Status (ISEI) gives an indication of the extent to which segregation by socio-economic levels occurs between schools. An added advantage of aggregation is that missing data items are reduced to zero at the school level. The variables in the student file that could provide useful school-level indicators include:

– School level International Socio-Economic Index of Occupational Status (ISEI or HISEI)

– Index of family wealth of the student body (WEALTH)

– Index of teacher support (TEACHSUP)

– Index of disciplinary climate (DISCLIMA)

– Index of teacher-student relations (STUDREL)

– Index of achievement press (ACHPRESS)

– Index of students' sense of belonging in the school (BELONG).

An example of a SPSS® syntax for aggregating ISEI is provided in Figure 6.

Figure 6

SPSS® syntax used to aggregate the International Socio-Economic Index of Occupational Status (ISEI) of the student level to the school level

```
get file='file with variable to be aggregated'.
sort by schoolid (a).
aggregate
    /outfile='new file to contain aggregate variable(s)'
    /break=schoolid
    /schisei = mean(isei).
*schisei is thus the aggregated isei.


get file='school file to which aggregate isei is to be matched'.
sort by schoolid (a).


*both files need to be sorted in ascending order by the variable on which they are matched.
*the match variable must be a unique identifier for the school and in the same format in both *files.
The variable schoolid is the match variable in this example. It was created by multiplying the *stratum
ID (stidstrt) by 1,000,000 and adding it to the school ID (stidsch) in both files.


match files
        /file=*
        /table='new file containing aggregate variable(s)'
        /by schoolid.


save outfile='new file containing original school file plus new aggregate variables'.
execute.
```

THE SCHOOL FILE

The responses to the school questionnaire

The school files contain the original variables collected through the school context questionnaire.

The names which are used to represent these variables in the international database are directly related to the international version of the school questionnaire. Each variable name consists of seven characters.

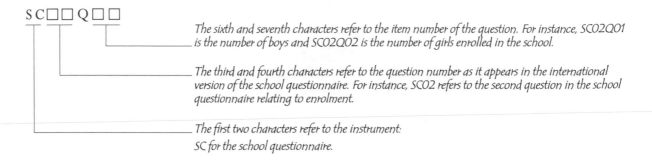

S C ☐ ☐ Q ☐ ☐

The sixth and seventh characters refer to the item number of the question. For instance, SCO2Q01 is the number of boys and SCO2Q02 is the number of girls enrolled in the school.

The third and fourth characters refer to the question number as it appears in the international version of the school questionnaire. For instance, SCO2 refers to the second question in the school questionnaire relating to enrolment.

The first two characters refer to the instrument:
SC for the school questionnaire.

The school weight

The school base weight, which has been adjusted for school non-response, is provided at the end of the school file. PISA uses an age sample instead of a grade sample. Additionally, the PISA sample of school in some countries included primary schools, lower secondary schools, upper secondary schools, or even special education schools. For these two reasons, it is difficult to conceptually define the school population, except this it is the population of schools with at least one 15-year-old student. While in some countries, the population of schools with 15-year-olds is similar to the population of secondary schools, in other countries, these two populations of schools are very different.

A recommendation is to analyse the school data at the student level. From a practical point of view, it means that the school data should to be imported into the student data file. From a theoretical point of view, while it is possible to estimate the percentages of schools following a specific school characteristic, it is not meaningful. Instead, the recommendation is to estimate the percentages of students following the same school characteristic. For instance, the percentages of private schools versus public schools will not be estimated, but the percentages of students attending a private school versus the percentage of students attending public schools will.

As school data will be imported in the student data file, the final weight and the 80 Fay's replicates will be used in a similar what to how they are used for the student data.

The school questionnaire indices

As in the student questionnaire data file, two kinds of indices were derived from the school questionnaire data.

Indices derived through a direct combination of the answers from the school questionnaire

These indices, derived from the school questionnaire, are mainly related to the school size, the computer environment of the school and school staffing.

– *School size (SCHLSIZE)*. This index represents the total enrolment in the school and is the sum of the number of boys (SC02Q01) and the number of girls (SC02Q02) enrolled in the school.

– *Percentage of girls (PCGIRLS)*. This index is the ratio between the number of girls and the total enrolment – number of boys (SC02Q01) plus number of girls (SC02Q02) – *i.e.*, the number of girls in the school divided by the total enrolment.

– *School type (SCHLTYPE)*. A school was classified as either public or private according to whether a public agency or a private entity had the ultimate power to make decisions concerning its affairs. It was based on SC03Q01 and SC04Q01 to SC04Q04. It was further divided into three categories[7]:

- *Government-independent private schools* were coded as 1, if the school principal reported that the school was controlled and managed by a non-governmental organisation (*e.g.*, a church, a trade union or a business enterprise) or if its governing board consisted mostly of members not selected by a public agency, where it received less than 50 per cent of its core funding from government agencies.

- *Government-dependent private schools* were coded as 2, if the school principal reported that the school was controlled and managed by a non-governmental organisation (*e.g.*, a church, a trade union or a business enterprise) or if its governing board consisted mostly of members not selected by a public agency, where it received 50 per cent or more of its core funding from government agencies.

- *Government or public schools* were coded as 3, if the school principal reported that the school was: controlled and managed directly by a public education authority or agency; or controlled and managed either by a government agency directly or by a governing body (council, committee, etc.), most of whose members were either appointed by a public authority or elected by public franchise.

– *Hours of schooling per year (TOTHRS)*. This index was derived from the information which principals provided on: the number of weeks in the school year for which the school operates; the number of <class periods> in the school week; and the number of teaching minutes in a single <class period>. It consists of the total number of 60-minute hours of schooling per year. It was based on the product of the three factors, SC06Q01, SC06Q02, SC06Q03, divided by 60.

– *Number of computers per student per school (RATCOMP)*. This index is the total number of computers in the school (SC13Q01), divided by the school size (SCHLSIZE).

– *Proportion of computers available to 15-year-olds (PERCOMP1)*. This index is the number of computers available to 15-year-old students (SC13Q02), divided by the total number of computers in the school (SC13Q01).

– *Proportion of computers available to teachers only (PERCOMP2)*. This index is the number of computers available only to teachers (SC13Q03), divided by the total number of computers in the school (SC13Q01).

---

7. For a definition of the types of schools, see OECD (1998, p. 422).

— *Proportion of computers available to the administrative staff (PERCOMP3)*. This index is the total number of computers available only to the administrative staff (SC13Q04), divided by the total number of computers in the school (SC13Q01).

— *Proportion of computers with Internet access (PERCOMP4)*. This index is the number of computers connected to the Internet/World Wide Web (SC13Q05), divided by the total number of computers in the school (SC13Q01).

— *Proportion of computers on a local network (PERCOMP5)*. This index is the number of computers connected to a local area network (LAN, Intranet) (SC13Q06), divided by the total number of computers in the school (SC13Q01).

— *Student-teaching staff ratio (STRATIO)*. This index is the school size (SCHLSIZE) divided by the total number of teachers (SC14Q01+(0.5*SC14Q02), that is, part-time teachers contribute 0.5 and full-time teachers 1.0 to the total number of teachers). This rule applies to all indices based on question SC14.

— *Proportion of teachers with a third level qualification [ISCED 5A] (PROPQUAL)*. This index is the total number of teachers who have an <ISCED 5A> qualification in <pedagogy> (SC14Q03+(0.5*SC14Q04)) divided by the total number of teachers (SC14Q01+(0.5*SC14Q02)).

— *Proportion of teachers who are certified by the appropriate authority (PROPCERT)*. This index is the total number of teachers fully certified as teachers by <the appropriate authority> (SC14Q05+(0.5*SC14Q06)) divided by the total number of teachers (SC14Q01+(0.5*SC14Q02)).

— *Proportion of <language of assessment> teachers who have a third level qualification (ISCED 5A) (PROPREAD)*. This index is the total number of <language of assessment> teachers who have a third level qualification (SC14Q09+(0.5*SC14Q10)) divided by the total number of teachers (SC14Q01 + (0.5*SC14Q02)).

— *Proportion of mathematics teachers who have a third level qualification (ISCED 5A) (PROPMATH)*. This index is the total number of mathematics teachers who have a third level qualification (SC14Q13+(0.5*SC14Q14)) divided by the total number of teachers (SC14Q01 + (0.5*SC14Q02)).

— *Proportion of science teachers who have a third level qualification (ISCED 5A) (PROPSCIE)*. This index is the total number of science teachers who have a third level qualification (SC14Q17+(0.5*SC14Q18)) divided by the total number of teachers (SC14Q01 + (0.5*SC14Q02)).

Weighted likelihood estimate indices

The following indices from the school questionnaire were derived using the weighted estimate method (Warm, 1985):

— *Index of the quality of schools' educational resources (SCMATEDU)*. This index was derived from school principals' reports on the extent to which learning by 15-year-olds in their school was hindered by: lack of instructional material; not enough computers for instruction; lack of instructional materials in the library; lack of multi-media resources for instruction; inadequate science laboratory equipment; and, inadequate facilities for the fine arts. It was based on questions SC11Q04 to SC11Q09. This index was inverted during reporting so that low values indicate a low quality of educational resources (OECD, 2001)

— **Index of the quality of schools' physical infrastructure (SCMATBUI)**. This index was derived from principals' reports on the extent to which learning by 15-year-olds in their school was hindered by: poor condition of buildings; poor heating and cooling and/or lighting systems; and, lack of instructional space (*e.g.*, in classrooms). It was based on questions SC11Q01 to SC11Q03. This index was inverted during reporting so that low values indicate a low quality of physical infrastructure (OECD, 2001).

— **Index of teacher shortage (TCSHORT)**. This index was derived from principals' views on how much learning by 15-year-old students was hindered by: shortage or inadequacy of teachers in general and shortage of teachers in the <language of assessment>, mathematics or science. It was based on questions SC21Q01 TO SC21Q04. This index was inverted during reporting so that low values indicate problems with teacher shortage (OECD, 2001).

— **Index of principals' perceptions of teacher-related factors affecting school climate (TEACBEHA)**. This index was derived from principals' reports on the extent to which the learning by 15-year-olds was hindered by: low expectations of teachers; poor student-teacher relations; teachers not meeting individual students' needs; teacher absenteeism; staff resisting change; teachers being too strict with students; and students not being encouraged to achieve their full potential. It was based on questions SC19Q01, SC19Q03, SC19Q07, SC19Q08, SC19Q11, SC19Q14 and SC19Q16. This index was inverted during reporting so that lower values indicate a poorer disciplinary climate (OECD, 2001).

— **Index of principals' perceptions of student-related factors affecting school climate (STUDBEHA)**. This index was derived from principals' reports on the extent to which learning by 15-year-olds in their school was hindered by: student absenteeism; disruption of classes by students; students skipping classes; students lacking respect for teachers; the use of alcohol or illegal drugs; and students intimidating or bullying other students. It was based on questions SC19Q02, SC19Q06, SC19Q09, SC19Q10, SC19Q13 and SC19Q15. This index was inverted during reporting so that low values indicate a poorer disciplinary climate (OECD, 2001).

— **Index of principals' perceptions of teachers' morale and commitment (TCMORALE)**. This index was derived from the extent to which school principals agreed with the following statements: the morale of the teachers in this school is high; teachers work with enthusiasm; teachers take pride in this school; and, teachers value academic achievement. It was based on questions SC20Q01 to SC20Q04.

— **Index of school autonomy (SCHAUTON)**. School principals were asked to report whether teachers, department heads, the school principal, an appointed or elected board or an education authority at a higher level had the main responsibility for: appointing teachers; dismissing teachers; establishing teachers' starting salaries; determining teachers' salary increases; formulating school budgets; allocating budgets within the school; establishing student disciplinary policies; establishing student assessment policies; approving students for admittance to school; choosing which textbooks to use; determining course content; and deciding which courses were offered. The PISA index of school autonomy was derived from the number of categories that principals classified as not being a school responsibility. It was based on questions SC22Q01 to SC22Q12. This index was inverted during reporting so that high values indicate a high degree of autonomy.

– *Index of teacher autonomy (TCHPARTI)*. School principals were asked to report whether teachers, department heads, the school principal, an appointed or elected board or an education authority at a higher level had the main responsibility for: appointing teachers; dismissing teachers; establishing teachers' starting salaries; determining teachers' salary increases; formulating school budgets; allocating budgets within the school; establishing student disciplinary policies; establishing student assessment policies; approving students for admittance to school; choosing which textbooks to use; determining course content; and deciding which courses were offered. The PISA index of teacher autonomy was derived from the number of categories that principals classified as being mainly the responsibility of teachers. It was based on questions SC22Q01 to SC22Q12.

These indices, based on weighted estimates (Warm, 1985), were standardised to have a mean of 0 and a standard deviation of 1 at the international level using the same procedures as were applied to the performance variables, *i.e.*, each OECD country, except the Netherlands[8], contributed equally to the standardisation.

---

8. Response rate too low to ensure comparability (Annex A3, OECD (2001)).

THE FILE WITH THE STUDENT TEST DATA

The file with the test data (*filename: INTCOGN TXT*) contains individual students' responses to all items used for the international item calibration and in the generation of the plausible values. All item responses included in this file have a one-digit format, which contains the score for the student on that item.

The PISA items are organised into units. Each unit consists of a piece of text or related texts, followed by one or more questions. Each unit is identified by a short label and by a long label. The units' short labels consist of four characters. The first character is R, M or S respectively for reading, mathematics or science. The three next characters indicate the unit name. For example, R083 is a reading unit called 'Household'. The full item label (usually seven-digit) represents each particular question within a unit. Thus items within a unit have the same initial four characters: all items in the unit 'Household' begin with 'R083', plus a question number: for example, the third question in the 'Household' unit is R083Q03.

Users may notice that the question numbers in some cases are not sequential, and in other cases, that question numbers are missing. The initial item numbering was done before the field trial, with some changes occurring after it (the field trial took place a year before the main assessment). For example, during the development of the main study instruments, some items were re-ordered within a unit, while others were deleted from the item pool.

In this file, the items are sorted by domain and alphabetically by short label within domain. This means that the mathematics items appear at the beginning of the file, followed by the reading items and then the science items. Within domains, units with smaller numeric IDs appear before those with larger IDs, and within each unit, the first question will precede the second, and so on.

Recoding of the assessment items

Some of the items needed to be recoded prior to the national and international scaling processes.

— Double-digit coded items (mathematics and science only) were truncated by retaining only the first digit, which corresponds to the score initially assigned to the item.

— Other items were recoded and/or combined. These items have been re-labelled. The character "T" was added to the end of the previous short label for such items.

— Numerical variables were recoded into scores, *i.e.*, incorrect answer (0), correct answer (1), missing answer (9) or not applicable (7).

— Some questions consisted of several true/false or yes/no items. Two questions were also composed of several multiple choice items (R088Q04 and R099Q03). These items were combined into new variables. The new codes correspond to the number of correct answers on the subset of items.

— Finally, five items, which comprised a subset of items (R119Q09, R122Q01, R216Q03, R219Q01 and M192Q01), were combined to form new variables. The combined codes correspond to the number of correct answers to each of the sub-items included in these five items.

National item deletions

Assessment data were initially scaled by country, and item parameter estimates were analysed across countries. During the item adjudication process, some items were flagged for particular countries and a consultation process took place to perform additional checks on these so-called "dodgy items". This consultation led to the deletion of a few of them at the national level. These deleted items, identified in Figure 7, were recoded as *not applicable* and were not included in either the international scaling or the generation of plausible values.

Figure 7

Items deleted for a particular country

Country	Item name	Country	Item name
Austria	M155Q03	Korea	R237Q03
Austria	R055Q03	Korea	R246Q02
Austria	S133Q04T	Mexico	R040Q02
Belgium, Dutch version	R076Q05	Netherlands	R076Q05
Belgium, Dutch version	R100Q05	Netherlands	R100Q05
Brazil	M033Q01	Netherlands	S268Q02T
Canada, French version	R101Q08	Poland	R099Q04B
England	R076Q03	Russian Federation	R091Q05
England	R076Q04	Spain	R227Q01
Germany	R055Q03	Sweden	R091Q07B
Germany	S133Q04T	Switzerland, German version	M155Q01
Greece	R040Q02	Switzerland, German version	M155Q03
Hungary	R119Q04	Switzerland, German version	M155Q04
Iceland	R236Q01	Switzerland, German version	R055Q03
Iceland	S268Q02T	Switzerland, German version	R076Q03
Italy	R040Q06	Switzerland, German version	R091Q05
Italy	R219Q01T	Switzerland, German version	R111q06B
Japan	M155Q01	Switzerland, German version	R239Q02
Korea	R102Q04A	Switzerland, German version	S133Q04T
Korea	R216Q02	Switzerland, Italian version	S268Q06

International scores assigned to the items

The final scores allocated to the different categories are presented in Appendix 8. The codes are grouped according to the scores they were assigned for the final international calibration.

MODIFICATION OF THE INTERNATIONAL DATABASE

The PISA 2000 Initial Report analyses were performed on a preliminary version of the international database. This preliminary version was used extensively by the National Project Managers in the participating countries for writing their national reports.

During the data analysis phase, a few National Project Managers identified some remaining errors and submitted some requests for recoding of the original data. This section describes the modifications introduced in the preliminary version. Some of these modifications will have slight effects on the results published in the initial report.

Student questionnaire data

The following national modifications relating to the student questionnaire data were implemented to the international database:

- **Latvia**: recoding to "not applicable" of questions ST41Q01 to ST41Q06;

- **Netherlands**: recoding of about 300 records for question ST25Q01 and fewer than 100 records for question ST17Q01;

- **Portugal**: recoding to "not applicable" all records for question ST01Q01;

- **Switzerland**: recoding of fewer than 100 records for question ST17Q01;

- **Sweden**: recoding of fewer than 100 records for questions ST41Q04 to ST41Q06.

School questionnaire data

The following national modifications relating to the school questionnaire data were implemented to the international database:

- **Australia**: recoding of fewer than 100 records for question SC02Q01, SC02Q02, and SC05Q01 to SC05Q14; recoding to "not applicable" of question SC07Q02.

- **Ireland**: recoding of fewer than 10 records for question SC02Q01, SC02Q02 and SC14Q01 to SC14Q18.

MAKING COMPARISONS

To test whether the means for two sub-groups (A and B) of students are different a t-test needs to be performed. The formula for the t-test is:

$$T = \frac{(\hat{\mu}_A - \hat{\mu}_B)}{\sqrt{\hat{\sigma}^2_{(\hat{\mu}_A - \hat{\mu}_B)}}}$$

where $\hat{\mu}_A$ is the estimated mean of group A, $\hat{\mu}_B$ is the estimated mean of group B, and $\hat{\sigma}^2$ is the estimated sampling variance for the difference in the means. The null hypothesis of equal means is rejected at the α level if $|T| > t_v(\alpha)$, where $t_v(\alpha)$ is the α critical value for the t distribution with v degrees of freedom.

In general

$$\hat{\sigma}^2_{(\hat{\mu}_A - \hat{\mu}_B)} = \hat{\sigma}^2_{(\hat{\mu}_A)} + \hat{\sigma}^2_{(\hat{\mu}_B)} - 2\text{cov}(\hat{\mu}_A, \hat{\mu}_B)$$

where $\hat{\sigma}^2_{(\hat{\mu}_A)}$ is the sampling variance for the estimated mean of group A, $\hat{\sigma}^2_{(\hat{\mu}_B)}$ is the sampling variance for the estimated mean of group B, and $\text{cov}(\hat{\mu}_A, \hat{\mu}_B)$ is the sampling covariance for the estimates of the two means. That is, the sampling variance for the difference between two means is equal to the sampling variance on the first mean (Group A), plus the sampling variance on the second mean (Group B), minus two times the covariance between the two means. If the two samples are independent, this covariance is 0, and the sampling variance of the difference simplifies to be the sum of the sampling variance for the estimates of the performance for each of the two groups

Dependent versus independent samples

If the *samples are independent*, as is the case for countries in the PISA, the sampling variance for the difference between two countries will be the sum of their respective sampling variances.

If the *samples are not independent*, the covariance will need to be computed to accurately estimate the sampling variance of the difference. Two examples of dependent samples are: *i)* the sample of boys and the sample of girls within a particular country, and *ii)* the country sample and the OECD sample as the country sample contributes to the OECD parameter estimates (*e.g.,* when comparing the country mean estimate with the OECD average).

When samples are not independent, a way to estimate the sampling variance for the difference is to use the Fay's replicates (variables W_FSTR1-W_FSTR80) included in the international database. In the case of comparing a country mean estimate with the OECD mean estimate, the final estimate for the difference will be the difference between the country estimate and the OECD estimate, using the student final weight, *i.e.* W_FTSUWT. To compute the sampling variance for the difference, it will be necessary to compute the difference for each replicate; then use these 80 estimates for the difference to compute the sampling variance on the difference, as mentioned on page 19 of this manual. Another way to compute the sampling variance for the difference is to use the cell function in WesVar®.

Note: It is worth noting that the sampling variance for the difference between two independent samples can also be computed in WesVar®, using the replicates. But, given that a small covariance may be observed by chance, the results will be slightly different than when using the formulae for two independent samples.

The Bonferroni Adjustment

In the publication *Knowledge and Skills for Life – First Results from PISA 2000 (OECD, 2001)* the Bonferroni adjustment was used in the test of significance in the multiple comparison tables and in the figures comparing each country mean estimate with the mean estimate of other countries used (Figure 2.4, Figure 3.2, Figure 3.6, Table 2.2a, Table 2.2b, and Table 2.2c). The Bonferroni adjustment was not applied to the tests of significance included in any other tables or figures, including those that compare the country mean estimate and the OECD mean estimates.

In the table of multiple comparisons of achievement, the reader is more likely to compare one country with each of the other countries one at a time. Therefore, the Bonferroni adjustment is based on 31 comparisons (that is, one country with the other 31 countries) and not 496 comparisons (that is, all possible pairwise comparisons (32*31)/2). With a type I error rate of 0.05, the critical value adjusted for 31 comparisons is approximately equal to 3.154, instead of 1.960.

ADDITIONAL TECHNICAL INFORMATION AND GLOSSARY

Calculation of correlation using plausible values

Let us suppose that one is interested in the correlation between the student reading ability, denoted X, and a context variable Y, collected through the student questionnaire. The correlation between X and Y, denoted $r*(X,Y)$, should be computed for each of the five plausible values. The correlation that has to be reported will be the average of the five computed correlations:

$$r*(X,Y) = \frac{1}{5} \sum_{m=1}^{5} \hat{r}_m,$$

where $\hat{r}_m$ is the estimate of r computed using the mth plausible value.

The final estimate of r is the average of the estimates computed using each plausible value in turn. If U_m is the sampling variance for $\hat{r}_m$ then the sampling variance of $r*$ is:

$$V = U* + (1 + M^{-1})B_M,$$

where $U* = \frac{1}{m} \sum_{m=1}^{M} U_m$ and $B_M = \frac{1}{M-1} \sum_{m=1}^{M} (\hat{r}_m - r*)^2$.

An α–% confidence interval for $r*$ is $r* \pm t_V [(1-\alpha)/2]V^{1/2}$ where $t_v(s)$ is the s percentile of the t–distribution with V degrees of freedom. $V = \dfrac{1}{\dfrac{f^2_M}{M-1} + \dfrac{(1-f_M)^2}{d}}$, $f_M = (1 + M^{-1})B_M / V$

and d is the degrees of freedom that would have applied if θ_n had been observed. In PISA the value of d will be equal to 80.

It is worth noting that the use of one plausible value will provide unbiased estimates of population parameters. However, the standard error estimated from the use of just one plausible value will contain the sampling variance component and not the measurement variance. It will therefore slightly underestimate the total uncertainty in the estimate.[9]

Codebook

A codebook is a document that identifies the variables and all possible values associated with them. In addition to the name of the variable, it also shows the variable label, all possible responses (*i.e.*, in the case of multiple choice items it shows the values for all alternatives and the full label of each alternative), type of variable (*e.g.* string or numeric) and the columns where the values are shown in the actual data file.

---

9. B_M cannot be computed if just one plausible value is used.

Compendia

Compendia include a set of tables showing statistics for every item included in the questionnaires, and the relationship with performance. The tables show the percentage of students per category of response and the performance for the group of students in each category of response.

Double-digit coding

Students' responses could give valuable information about their ideas and thinking, besides being correct or incorrect. The marking guides for mathematics and science included a system of two-digit coding for marking so that the frequency of various types of correct and incorrect responses could be recoded. The first digit is the actual score. The second digit is used to categorise the different kinds of responses on the basis of the strategies used by the student to answer the item. There are two main advantages of using double-digit codes. Firstly, more information can be collected about students' misconceptions, common errors, and different approaches to solving problems. Secondly, double-digit coding allows a more structured way of presenting the codes, clearly indicating the hierarchical levels of groups of codes. The assessment data files including the second digit were available to national centres.

ISO 3166

For International Standardization Organization (ISO) country codes, see _ftp://ftp.ripe.net/iso3166-countrycodes_.

Replication methodology for calculation of variance

The approach used for calculating sampling variances is known as Balanced Repeated Replication (BRR), or Balanced Half-Samples. A particular variant, known as Fay's method, has been used.

The variance estimator is:

$$V_{BRR}(X*) = \frac{1}{T(1-K)^2} \sum_{t=1}^{T} \{(X*_t - X*)^2\},$$

where X* is the estimate of a given statistic from the full sample, $V*_t$ a set of T replicate estimates and K the Fay's coefficient. For PISA 2000, 80 replicates were computed and the Fay's coefficient was set to K = 0.5. Therefore, the factor $\frac{1}{T(1-K)^2}$ is equal to $\frac{1}{20}$.

SAS®

SAS® is a statistical package. For further information: _http://www.sas.com_.

SPSS®

SPSS® is a statistical package. For further information: _http://www.spss.com_.

Student weights

Calculation of student weights

The *weight*, W_{ij}, for student j in school i can be expressed in the following form:

$$W_{ij} = f_{1i} f_{2i} f_{1i}^A w_{2ij} w_{1i}, \text{ where}$$

w_{1i} is given as the reciprocal of the probability of inclusion of school i in the sample;

w_{2ij} is given as the reciprocal of the probability of selection of student j from within the selected school i;

f_{1i} is an adjustment factor to compensate for non-participation by other schools that are somewhat similar in nature to school i (not already compensated for by the participation of replacement schools);

f_{1i}^A is an adjustment factor to compensate for the fact that, in some countries, in some schools only 15-year-old students who are enrolled in the modal grade for 15-year-olds were included in the assessment; and

f_{2i} is an adjustment factor to compensate for the absence of performance scale scores from some sampled students within school i (who were not excluded).

Explanation of weight adjustment factors associated with the special education (SE) booklet

Let us suppose that 1,000 students were assessed in a country. Suppose that nine hundred of these students were assessed with one of the nine rotated booklets, as shown in Figure 8, and the remaining 100 students were assessed with the SE booklet. Mathematics materials were included in booklets 1, 3, 5, 8, 9 and in the SE booklet, and science materials were included in booklets 2, 4, 6, 8, 9 and in the SE booklet.

Figure 8

Example of numbers of students assessed in the three domains, by booklet

Booklet	Reading	Mathematics	Science
1	100	100	
2	100		100
3	100	100	
4	100		100
5	100	100	
6	100		100
7	100		
8	100	100	100
9	100	100	100
SE	100	100	100

One tenth of the students were assessed with the SE booklet. If mathematics or science data are analysed with the reading weights, then the students assessed with the SE booklets will represent one sixth (100 out of 600), while they should represent one tenth.

Thus, the mathematics weight factor is given as:

1.0 for each student assigned the special education booklet;

1.8 for each student assigned one of the nine rotated booklets that contain mathematics material;

0.0 for each student assigned one of the nine rotated booklets that contain no mathematics material.

If these adjustment factors are applied to the data presented in the previous example, students assessed with booklet 1 will count for 180 students, students assessed with booklet 3 will also count for 180 students, and so on. On the other hand, students assessed with the SE booklet will still count for 100. Therefore, students assessed with the SE booklet will represent one tenth.

Similarly, the science weight factor is given as:

1.0 for each student assigned the special education booklet;

1.8 for each student assigned one of the nine rotated booklets that contain science material;

0.0 for each student assigned one of the nine rotated booklets that contain no science material.

WesVar®

WesVar® is a statistical package that computes estimates and their variance estimates from survey data using replication methods. The information generated can then be used to estimate sampling errors for different types of survey statistics. It can be used in conjunction with a wide range of complex sample designs, including multistage, stratified, and unequal probability samples. For further information: _http://www.westat.com/wesvar_.

FURTHER READING

References

Baumert, J., Gruehn, S., Heyn, S., Köller, O. and **Schnabel, K.U.** (1997), *Bildungsverläufe und Psychosoziale Entwicklung im Jugendalter (BIJU): Dokumentation - Band 1,* Max-Planck-Institut für Bildungsforschung, Berlin.

Baumert, J., Heyn. S. and **Köller, O.** (1994), *Das Kieler Lernstrategien-Inventar (KSI),* Institut für die Pädagogik der Naturwissenschaften an der Universität Kiel, Kiel.

Eignor, D., Taylor, C., Kirsch, I. and **Jamieson, J.** (1998), *Development of a Scale for Assessing the Level of Computer Familiarity of TOEFL Students,* TOEFL Research Report No. 60, Educational Testing Service, Princeton, NJ.

Ganzeboom, H.B.G., De Graaf, P. and **Treiman, D.J.** (with **De Leeuw, J.**) (1992), "A standard international socio-economic index of occupational status", *Social Science Research,* Vol. 21(1), pp. 1-56.

Marsh, H. W., Shavelson, R.J. and **Byrne, B.M.** (1992), "A multidimensional, hierarchical self-concept", in R. P. Lipka and T. M. Brinthaupt (Eds.), *Studying the Self: Self-perspectives across the life-span,* State University of New York Press, Albany.

OECD (1998), *Education at a glance - OECD indicators,* Paris.

OECD (1999*a*), *Classifying educational programmes: Manual for ISCED-97 implementation in OECD countries,* Paris.

OECD (1999*b*), *Measuring student knowledge and skills: A new framework for assessment,* Paris.

OECD (2000), *Measuring student knowledge and skills: The PISA 2000 assessment of reading, mathematical and scientific literacy,* Paris.

OECD (2001), *Knowledge and skills for life: First results from PISA 2000,* Paris.

OECD (2002), *Sample tasks from the PISA 2000 assessment: Reading, mathematical and scientific literacy,* Paris.

Owens, L. and **Barnes, J.** (1992), *Learning Preferences Scales,* ACER, Victoria, Australia.

Warm, T.A. (1985), "Weighted maximum likelihood estimation of ability in Item Response Theory using tests of finite length", *Technical Report CGI-TR-85-08,* U.S. Cost Guard Institute, Oklahoma City.

Westat (2000), *WesVar complex samples 4.0.* Rockville, MD.

Other relevant publications

OECD (2002, forthcoming), *PISA 2000 Technical Report,* Paris.

APPENDIX 1 *STUDENT QUESTIONNAIRE*

| ST01Q01 | Q 1 | On what date were you born? |
| ST01Q02 | | *(Please write in the day, month and year you were born.)* |

<table>
<tr><td>ST01Q03</td><td></td><td colspan="3"><_____ _____ 198 ____></td></tr>
<tr><td></td><td></td><td>Day</td><td>Month</td><td>Year</td></tr>
</table>

| ST02Q01 | Q 2 | What <grade> are you in? | _____ <grade> |

| ST03Q01 | Q 3 | Are you <female> or <male>? |

<Female>   <Male>
❏₁   ❏₂

Q 4   Who usually lives at <home> with you?

(Please <tick> only one box on each row.)

			Yes	*No*
ST04Q01		a) Mother	❏₁	❏₂
ST04Q02		b) Other female guardian (*e.g.*, stepmother or foster mother)	❏₁	❏₂
ST04Q03		c) Father	❏₁	❏₂
ST04Q04		d) Other male guardian (*e.g.*, stepfather or foster father)	❏₁	❏₂
ST04Q05		e) Brother(s) (including stepbrothers)	❏₁	❏₂
ST04Q06		f) Sister(s) (including stepsisters)	❏₁	❏₂
ST04Q07		g) Grandparent(s)	❏₁	❏₂
ST04Q08		h) Others	❏₁	❏₂

Q 5   How many brothers and sisters do you have?

(Please <tick> only one box on each row. When appropriate, remember to <tick> the 'None' box.)

			None	*One*	*Two*	*Three*	*Four or more*
ST05Q01		a) Older than you	❏₁	❏₂	❏₃	❏₄	❏₅
ST05Q02		b) Younger than you	❏₁	❏₂	❏₃	❏₄	❏₅
ST05Q03		c) Same age as you	❏₁	❏₂	❏₃	❏₄	❏₅

ST06Q01	**Q 6**	**What is your mother currently doing?**

(Please <tick> only one box.)

Working full-time <for pay>   ❏₁

Working part-time <for pay>   ❏₂

Not working, but looking for a job   ❏₃

Other (*e.g.* home duties, retired)   ❏₄

ST07Q01	**Q 7**	**What is your father currently doing?**

(Please <tick> only one box.)

Working full-time <for pay>   ❏₁

Working part-time <for pay>   ❏₂

Not working, but looking for a job   ❏₃

Other (*e.g.* home duties, retired)   ❏₄

Q 8   **What is your mother's main job?** (*e.g.*, <School teacher, nurse, sales manager>)
If she is not working now, please tell us her last main job.

Please write in the job title --

ST09Q01	**Q 9**	**What does your mother do in her main job?**

(e.g., <Teaches high school students, cares for patients, manages a sales team>)
If she is not working now, please tell us her last main job.

Please use a sentence to describe the kind of work she does or did in that job

----

Q 10   **What is your father's main job?** (*e.g.*, <School teacher, carpenter, sales manager>)
If he is not working now, please tell us his last main job.

Please write in the job title --

ST11Q01	**Q 11**	**What does your father do in his main job?**

(*e.g.*, <Teaches high school students, builds houses, manages a sales team>)
If he is not working now, please tell us his last main job.

Please use a sentence to describe the kind of work he does or did in that job

----

ST12Q01	**Q 12**	**Did your mother complete <ISCED 3A>?**

(Please <tick> only one box.)

No, she did not go to school .... $\Box_1$

No, she completed <ISCED level 1> only .... $\Box_2$

No, she completed <ISCED level 2> only .... $\Box_3$

No, she completed <ISCED level 3B or 3C> only .... $\Box_4$

Yes, she completed <ISCED level 3A> .... $\Box_5$

ST13Q01	**Q 13**	**Did your father complete <ISCED 3A>?**

(Please <tick> only one box.)

No, he did not go to school .... $\Box_1$

No, he completed <ISCED level 1> only .... $\Box_2$

No, he completed <ISCED level 2> only .... $\Box_3$

No, he completed <ISCED level 3B or 3C> only .... $\Box_4$

Yes, he completed <ISCED level 3A> .... $\Box_5$

ST14Q01	**Q 14**	**Did your mother complete <ISCED 5A, 5B, 6>?**

(Please <tick> only one box.)

<u>*Yes*</u>   <u>*No*</u>

$\Box_1$ $\Box_2$

ST15Q01	**Q 15**	**Did your father complete <ISCED 5A, 5B, 6>?**

(Please <tick> only one box.)

<u>*Yes*</u>   <u>*No*</u>

$\Box_1$ $\Box_2$

	Q 16	**In what country were you and your parents born?**

(Please <tick> only one box on each row.)

		<u>*<Country of test>*</u>	<u>*Another Country*</u>
ST16Q01	a) You	$\Box_1$	$\Box_2$
ST16Q02	b) Mother	$\Box_1$	$\Box_2$
ST16Q03	c) Father	$\Box_1$	$\Box_2$

ST17Q01 **Q 17** **What language do you speak at home most of the time?**

(Please <tick> only one box.)

<Test language>	$\square_1$
<Other official national languages>	$\square_2$
<Other national dialects or languages>	$\square_3$
<Other languages>	$\square_4$

Q 18 **During the past year, how often have you participated in these activities?**

(Please <tick> only one box on each row.)

		Never or hardly ever	Once or twice a year	About 3 or 4 times a year	More than 4 times a year
ST18Q01	a) Gone to the <pictures>.	$\square_1$	$\square_2$	$\square_3$	$\square_4$
ST18Q02	b) Visited a museum or art gallery.	$\square_1$	$\square_2$	$\square_3$	$\square_4$
ST18Q03	c) Attended a popular music concert.	$\square_1$	$\square_2$	$\square_3$	$\square_4$
ST18Q04	d) Attended an opera, ballet or classical symphony concert.	$\square_1$	$\square_2$	$\square_3$	$\square_4$
ST18Q05	e) Watched live theatre.	$\square_1$	$\square_2$	$\square_3$	$\square_4$
ST18Q06	f) Attended sporting events.	$\square_1$	$\square_2$	$\square_3$	$\square_4$

Q 19 **In general, how often do your parents:**

(Please <tick> only one box on each row.)

		Never or hardly ever	A few times a year	About once a month	Several times a month	Several times a week
ST19Q01	a) discuss political or social issues with you?	$\square_1$	$\square_2$	$\square_3$	$\square_4$	$\square_5$
ST19Q02	b) discuss books, films or television programmes with you?	$\square_1$	$\square_2$	$\square_3$	$\square_4$	$\square_5$
ST19Q03	c) listen to classical music with you?	$\square_1$	$\square_2$	$\square_3$	$\square_4$	$\square_5$
ST19Q04	d) discuss how well you are doing at school?	$\square_1$	$\square_2$	$\square_3$	$\square_4$	$\square_5$
ST19Q05	e) eat <the main meal> with you around a table?	$\square_1$	$\square_2$	$\square_3$	$\square_4$	$\square_5$
ST19Q06	f) spend time just talking to you?	$\square_1$	$\square_2$	$\square_3$	$\square_4$	$\square_5$

Q 20 How often do the following people work with you on your <schoolwork>?

(Please <tick> only one box on each row.)

		Never or hardly ever	A few times a year	About once a month	Several times a month	Several times a week
ST20Q01	a) Your mother	☐₁	☐₂	☐₃	☐₄	☐₅
ST20Q02	b) Your father	☐₁	☐₂	☐₃	☐₄	☐₅
ST20Q03	c) Your brothers and sisters	☐₁	☐₂	☐₃	☐₄	☐₅
ST20Q04	d) Grandparents	☐₁	☐₂	☐₃	☐₄	☐₅
ST20Q05	e) Other relations	☐₁	☐₂	☐₃	☐₄	☐₅
ST20Q06	f) Friends of your parents	☐₁	☐₂	☐₃	☐₄	☐₅

Q 21 In your home, do you have:

(Please <tick> only one box on each row.)

		Yes	No
ST21Q01	a) a dishwasher?	☐₁	☐₂
ST21Q02	b) a room of your own?	☐₁	☐₂
ST21Q03	c) educational software?	☐₁	☐₂
ST21Q04	d) a link to the Internet?	☐₁	☐₂
ST21Q05	e) a dictionary?	☐₁	☐₂
ST21Q06	f) a quiet place to study?	☐₁	☐₂
ST21Q07	g) a desk for study?	☐₁	☐₂
ST21Q08	h) text books?	☐₁	☐₂
ST21Q09	i) classic literature (*e.g.*, <Shakespeare>)?	☐₁	☐₂
ST21Q10	j) books of poetry?	☐₁	☐₂
ST21Q11	k) works of art (*e.g.*, paintings)?	☐₁	☐₂

Q 22 *How many* of these do you have at your home?

(Please <tick> only one box on each row.)

		None	One	Two	Three or more
ST22Q01	a) <Cellular> phone	☐₁	☐₂	☐₃	☐₄
ST22Q02	b) Television	☐₁	☐₂	☐₃	☐₄
ST22Q03	c) Calculator	☐₁	☐₂	☐₃	☐₄
ST22Q04	d) Computer	☐₁	☐₂	☐₃	☐₄
ST22Q05	e) Musical instrument (*e.g.*, piano, violin)	☐₁	☐₂	☐₃	☐₄
ST22Q06	f) Motor car	☐₁	☐₂	☐₃	☐₄
ST22Q07	g) Bathroom	☐₁	☐₂	☐₃	☐₄

Q 23 During the last three years, have you attended any of these special courses _at your school_ to improve your results?

(Please <tick> only one box on each row.)

		No, never	Yes, sometimes	Yes, regularly
ST23Q01	a) <Extension> or additional courses	☐₁	☐₂	☐₃
ST23Q02	b) <Remedial> courses in <test language>	☐₁	☐₂	☐₃
ST23Q03	c) <Remedial> courses in other subjects	☐₁	☐₂	☐₃
ST23Q04	d) Training to improve your study skills	☐₁	☐₂	☐₃

Q 24 During the last three years, have you attended any of these special courses _outside of your school_ to improve your results?

(Please <tick> only one box on each row.)

		No, never	Yes, sometimes	Yes, regularly
ST24Q01	a) Courses in <test language>	☐₁	☐₂	☐₃
ST24Q02	b) Courses in other subjects	☐₁	☐₂	☐₃
ST24Q03	c) <Extension> or additional courses	☐₁	☐₂	☐₃
ST24Q04	d) <Remedial> courses in <test language>	☐₁	☐₂	☐₃
ST24Q05	e) <Remedial> courses in other subjects	☐₁	☐₂	☐₃
ST24Q06	f) Training to improve your study skills	☐₁	☐₂	☐₃
ST24Q07	g) <Private tutoring>	☐₁	☐₂	☐₃

Q 25 What <programme> are you in at school?

(Please <tick> only one box.)

ST25Q01	<ISCED 2A>	☐₁
	<ISCED 2B>	☐₂
	<ISCED 2C>	☐₃
	<ISCED 3A>	☐₄
	<ISCED 3B>	☐₅
	<ISCED 3C>	☐₆

Q 26 How often do these things happen in your <test language> lessons?

(Please <tick> only one box on each row.)

		Never	Some lessons	Most lessons	Every lesson
ST26Q01	a) The teacher has to wait a long time for students to <quieten down>.	☐₁	☐₂	☐₃	☐₄
ST26Q02	b) The teacher wants students to work hard.	☐₁	☐₂	☐₃	☐₄
ST26Q03	c) The teacher tells students that they can do better.	☐₁	☐₂	☐₃	☐₄
ST26Q04	d) The teacher does not like it when students deliver <careless> work.	☐₁	☐₂	☐₃	☐₄
ST26Q05	e) The teacher shows an interest in every student's learning.	☐₁	☐₂	☐₃	☐₄
ST26Q06	f) The teacher gives students an opportunity to express opinions.	☐₁	☐₂	☐₃	☐₄
ST26Q07	g) The teacher helps students with their work.	☐₁	☐₂	☐₃	☐₄
ST26Q08	h) The teacher continues teaching until the students understand.	☐₁	☐₂	☐₃	☐₄
ST26Q09	i) The teacher does a lot to help students.	☐₁	☐₂	☐₃	☐₄
ST26Q10	j) The teacher hclps students with their learning.	☐₁	☐₂	☐₃	☐₄
ST26Q11	k) The teacher checks students' homework.	☐₁	☐₂	☐₃	☐₄
ST26Q12	l) Students cannot work well.	☐₁	☐₂	☐₃	☐₄
ST26Q13	m) Students don't listen to what the teacher says.	☐₁	☐₂	☐₃	☐₄
ST26Q14	n) Students don't start working for a long time after the lesson begins.	☐₁	☐₂	☐₃	☐₄
ST26Q15	o) Students have to learn a lot.	☐₁	☐₂	☐₃	☐₄
ST26Q16	p) There is noise and disorder.	☐₁	☐₂	☐₃	☐₄
ST26Q17	q) At the start of class, more than five minutes are spent doing nothing.	☐₁	☐₂	☐₃	☐₄

Q 27   In the last full week you were in school, how many <class periods> did you spend in:

(Please write in the number of class periods.)

	Total number	Does this number apply for most of the school year

ST27Q01
ST27Q02   a) <test language>?   _____   Yes ❑₁   No ❑₂

ST27Q03
ST27Q04   b) <mathematics> <in total>?   _____   Yes ❑₁   No ❑₂

ST27Q05
ST27Q06   c) <science> <in total>?   _____   Yes ❑₁   No ❑₂

Q 28   On average, about how many students are in your:

(Please write in the average number of students in each class.)

	Average number

ST28Q01   a) <test language class(es)>?   _____

ST28Q02   b) <mathematics class(es)>?   _____

ST28Q03   c) <science class(es)>?   _____

Q 29   How many times in the previous two school weeks did you:

(Please <tick> only one box on each row.)

	None	1 or 2	3 or 4	5 or more
ST29Q01 a) miss school?	❑₁	❑₂	❑₃	❑₄
ST29Q02 b) <skip> classes?	❑₁	❑₂	❑₃	❑₄
ST29Q03 c) arrive late for school?	❑₁	❑₂	❑₃	❑₄

Q 30   How much do you disagree or agree with each of the following statements about teachers at your school?

(Please <tick> only one box on each row.)

	Strongly disagree	Disagree	Agree	Strongly agree
ST30Q01 a) Students get along well with most teachers.	❑₁	❑₂	❑₃	❑₄
ST30Q02 b) Most teachers are interested in students' well-being.	❑₁	❑₂	❑₃	❑₄
ST30Q03 c) Most of my teachers really listen to what I have to say.	❑₁	❑₂	❑₃	❑₄
ST30Q04 d) If I need extra help, I will receive it from my teachers.	❑₁	❑₂	❑₃	❑₄
ST30Q05 e) Most of my teachers treat me fairly.	❑₁	❑₂	❑₃	❑₄

Q 31 My school is a place where:

(Please <tick> only one box on each row.)

		Strongly disagree	Disagree	Agree	Strongly agree
ST31Q01	a) I feel like an outsider (or left out of things).	$\square_1$	$\square_2$	$\square_3$	$\square_4$
ST31Q02	b) I make friends easily.	$\square_1$	$\square_2$	$\square_3$	$\square_4$
ST31Q03	c) I feel like I belong.	$\square_1$	$\square_2$	$\square_3$	$\square_4$
ST31Q04	d) I feel awkward and out of place.	$\square_1$	$\square_2$	$\square_3$	$\square_4$
ST31Q05	e) other students seem to like me.	$\square_1$	$\square_2$	$\square_3$	$\square_4$
ST31Q06	f) I feel lonely.	$\square_1$	$\square_2$	$\square_3$	$\square_4$
ST31Q07	g) I do not want to go.	$\square_1$	$\square_2$	$\square_3$	$\square_4$
ST31Q08	h) I often feel bored.	$\square_1$	$\square_2$	$\square_3$	$\square_4$

Q 32 Please indicate how often each of these applies to you.

(Please <tick> only one box on each row.)

		Never	Sometimes	Most of the time	Always
ST32Q01	a) I complete my homework on time.	$\square_1$	$\square_2$	$\square_3$	$\square_4$
ST32Q02	b) I do my homework while watching television.	$\square_1$	$\square_2$	$\square_3$	$\square_4$
ST32Q03	c) My teachers grade my homework.	$\square_1$	$\square_2$	$\square_3$	$\square_4$
ST32Q04	d) I finish my homework during the school day.	$\square_1$	$\square_2$	$\square_3$	$\square_4$
ST32Q05	e) My teachers make useful comments on my homework.	$\square_1$	$\square_2$	$\square_3$	$\square_4$
ST32Q06	f) I am given interesting homework.	$\square_1$	$\square_2$	$\square_3$	$\square_4$
ST32Q07	g) My homework is counted as part of my <marks>.	$\square_1$	$\square_2$	$\square_3$	$\square_4$

Q 33 On average, how much time do you spend *each week* on homework and study in these subject areas?

(Please <tick> only one box on each row.)

When answering include time at the weekend too.

		No time	Less than 1 hour a week	Between 1 hour and 3 hours a week	3 hours or more a week
ST33Q01	a) <test language>	$\square_1$	$\square_2$	$\square_3$	$\square_4$
ST33Q02	b) <mathematics>	$\square_1$	$\square_2$	$\square_3$	$\square_4$
ST33Q03	c) <science>	$\square_1$	$\square_2$	$\square_3$	$\square_4$

Q 34 *Each day*, about how much time do you usually spend reading for enjoyment?

(Please <tick> only one box.)

ST34Q01

I do not read for enjoyment.	❏₁
30 minutes or less each day.	❏₂
More than 30 minutes to less than 60 minutes each day.	❏₃
1 to 2 hours each day.	❏₄
More than 2 hours each day.	❏₅

Q 35 How much do you disagree or agree with these statements about reading?

(Please <tick> only one box on each row.)

		Strongly disagree	Disagree	Agree	Strongly agree
ST35Q01	a) I read only if I have to.	❏₁	❏₂	❏₃	❏₄
ST35Q02	b) Reading is one of my favourite hobbies.	❏₁	❏₂	❏₃	❏₄
ST35Q03	c) I like talking about books with other people.	❏₁	❏₂	❏₃	❏₄
ST35Q04	d) I find it hard to finish books.	❏₁	❏₂	❏₃	❏₄
ST35Q05	e) I feel happy if I receive a book as a present.	❏₁	❏₂	❏₃	❏₄
ST35Q06	f) For me, reading is a waste of time.	❏₁	❏₂	❏₃	❏₄
ST35Q07	g) I enjoy going to a bookstore or a library.	❏₁	❏₂	❏₃	❏₄
ST35Q08	h) I read only to get information that I need.	❏₁	❏₂	❏₃	❏₄
ST35Q09	i) I cannot sit still and read for more than a few minutes.	❏₁	❏₂	❏₃	❏₄

Q 36 How often do you read these materials *because you want to*?

(Please <tick> only one box on each row.)

		Never or hardly ever	A few times a year	About once a month	Several times a month	Several times a week
ST36Q01	a) Magazines.	❏₁	❏₂	❏₃	❏₄	❏₅
ST36Q02	b) Comic books.	❏₁	❏₂	❏₃	❏₄	❏₅
ST36Q03	c) Fictions (novels, narratives, stories).	❏₁	❏₂	❏₃	❏₄	❏₅
ST36Q04	d) Non-fiction books.	❏₁	❏₂	❏₃	❏₄	❏₅
ST36Q05	e) Emails and Web pages.	❏₁	❏₂	❏₃	❏₄	❏₅
ST36Q06	f) Newspapers.	❏₁	❏₂	❏₃	❏₄	❏₅

Q 37 How many books are there in your home?

There are usually about <40 books per metre> of shelving. Do not include magazines.

(Please <tick> only one box.)

ST37Q01

None.	☐₁
1-10 books.	☐₂
11-50 books.	☐₃
51-100 books.	☐₄
101-250 books.	☐₅
251-500 books.	☐₆
More than 500 books.	☐₇

ST38Q01 **Q 38** How often do you borrow books to read for pleasure from a public or school library?

(Please <tick> only one box.)

Never or hardly ever.	☐₁
A few times per year.	☐₂
About once a month.	☐₃
Several times a month.	☐₄

Q 39 At your school, about how often do you use:

(Please <tick> only one box on each row.)

	Never or hardly ever	A few times a year	About once a month	Several times a month	Several times a week
ST39Q01 a) school library?	☐₁	☐₂	☐₃	☐₄	☐₅
ST39Q02 b) computers?	☐₁	☐₂	☐₃	☐₄	☐₅
ST39Q03 c) calculators?	☐₁	☐₂	☐₃	☐₄	☐₅
ST39Q04 d) Internet?	☐₁	☐₂	☐₃	☐₄	☐₅
ST39Q05 e) <science> laboratories?	☐₁	☐₂	☐₃	☐₄	☐₅

ST40Q01 **Q 40** What kind of job do you expect to have when you are about 30 years old?

Write the job title: --

Q 41 In your last school report, what <mark> did you receive in the following subjects?

ST41Q01   a) <Test language>   _____

ST41Q02   b) <Mathematics>   _____

ST41Q03   c) <Science>   _____

Q 41 In your last school report, how did your <mark> compare with the <pass mark> in each subject area?

(Please <tick> only one box on each row.)

	Above the <pass mark>	At the <pass mark>	Below the <pass mark>
ST41Q04 a) <Test language>	❑₁	❑₂	❑₃
ST41Q05 b) <Mathematics>	❑₁	❑₂	❑₃
ST41Q06 c) <Science>	❑₁	❑₂	❑₃

APPENDIX 2 *CROSS CURRICULUM COMPETENCIES QUESTIONNAIRE*

Q1 How often do these things apply to you?

(Please <tick> only one box on each row.)

		Almost never	Sometimes	Often	Almost always
CC01Q01	1) When I study, I try to memorise everything that might be covered.	❏₁	❏₂	❏₃	❏₄
CC01Q02	2) I'm certain I can understand the most difficult material presented in texts.	❏₁	❏₂	❏₃	❏₄
CC01Q03	3) When I study, I start by figuring out exactly what I need to learn.	❏₁	❏₂	❏₃	❏₄
CC01Q04	4) When I sit myself down to learn something really difficult, I can learn it.	❏₁	❏₂	❏₃	❏₄
CC01Q05	5) When I study, I memorise as much as possible.	❏₁	❏₂	❏₃	❏₄
CC01Q06	6) I study to increase my job opportunities.				
CC01Q07	7) When studying, I work as hard as possible.	❏₁	❏₂	❏₃	❏₄
CC01Q08	8) I'm confident I can understand the most complex material presented by the teacher.	❏₁	❏₂	❏₃	❏₄
CC01Q09	9) When I study, I try to relate new material to things I have learned in other subjects.	❏₁	❏₂	❏₃	❏₄
CC01Q10	10) When I study, I memorise all new material so that I can recite it.	❏₁	❏₂	❏₃	❏₄
CC01Q11	11) If I decide not to get any bad grades, I can really do it.	❏₁	❏₂	❏₃	❏₄
CC01Q12	12) When studying, I keep working even if the material is difficult.	❏₁	❏₂	❏₃	❏₄
CC11Q13	13) When I study, I force myself to check to see if I remember what I have learned.	❏₁	❏₂	❏₃	❏₄
CC11Q14	14) I study to ensure that my future will be financially secure.	❏₁	❏₂	❏₃	❏₄
CC01Q15	15) When I study, I practise by saying the material to myself over and over.	❏₁	❏₂	❏₃	❏₄
CC01Q16	16) If I decide not to get any problems wrong, I can really do it.	❏₁	❏₂	❏₃	❏₄
CC01Q17	17) When I study, I figure out how the information might be useful in the real world.	❏₁	❏₂	❏₃	❏₄

		Almost never	Sometimes	Often	Almost always
CC01Q18	18) I'm confident I can do an excellent job on assignments and tests.	$\square_1$	$\square_2$	$\square_3$	$\square_4$
CC01Q19	19) When I study, I try to figure out which concepts I still haven't really understood.	$\square_1$	$\square_2$	$\square_3$	$\square_4$
CC01Q20	20) When studying, I try to do my best to acquire the knowledge and skills taught.	$\square_1$	$\square_2$	$\square_3$	$\square_4$
CC01Q21	21) When I study, I try to understand the material better by relating it to things I already know.	$\square_1$	$\square_2$	$\square_3$	$\square_4$
CC01Q22	22) I study to get a good job.	$\square_1$	$\square_2$	$\square_3$	$\square_4$
CC01Q23	23) When I study, I make sure that I remember the most important things.	$\square_1$	$\square_2$	$\square_3$	$\square_4$
CC01Q24	24) If I want to learn something well, I can.	$\square_1$	$\square_2$	$\square_3$	$\square_4$
CC01Q25	25) When I study, I figure out how the material fits in with what I have already learned.	$\square_1$	$\square_2$	$\square_3$	$\square_4$
CC01Q26	26) I'm certain I can master the skills being taught.	$\square_1$	$\square_2$	$\square_3$	$\square_4$
CC01Q27	27) When I study, and I don't understand something I look for additional information to clarify this.	$\square_1$	$\square_2$	$\square_3$	$\square_4$
CC01Q28	28) When studying, I put forth my best effort.	$\square_1$	$\square_2$	$\square_3$	$\square_4$

Q2   **How much do you disagree or agree with each of the following?**

(Please <tick> only one box on each row.)

		Disagree	Disagree somewhat	Agreee Somewhat	Agree
CC02Q01	29) When I do mathematics, I sometimes get totally absorbed.	$\square_1$	$\square_2$	$\square_3$	$\square_4$
CC02Q02	30) I like to work with other students.	$\square_1$	$\square_2$	$\square_3$	$\square_4$
CC02Q03	31) I learn things quickly in most school subjects.	$\square_1$	$\square_2$	$\square_3$	$\square_4$
CC02Q04	32) I like to try to be better than other students.	$\square_1$	$\square_2$	$\square_3$	$\square_4$
CC02Q05	33) I'm hopeless in <test language> classes.	$\square_1$	$\square_2$	$\square_3$	$\square_4$
CC02Q06	34) Because reading is fun, I wouldn't want to give it up.	$\square_1$	$\square_2$	$\square_3$	$\square_4$
CC02Q07	35) I'm good at most school subjects.	$\square_1$	$\square_2$	$\square_3$	$\square_4$
CC02Q08	36) I learn most when I work with other students.	$\square_1$	$\square_2$	$\square_3$	$\square_4$

		Disagree	Disagree somewhat	Agreee Somewhat	Agree
CC02Q09	37) I learn things quickly in <test language> class.	❏₁	❏₂	❏₃	❏₄
CC02Q10	38) Because doing mathematics is fun, I wouldn't want to give it up.	❏₁	❏₂	❏₃	❏₄
CC02Q11	39) Trying to be better than others makes me work well.	❏₁	❏₂	❏₃	❏₄
CC02Q12	40) I get good marks in mathematics.	❏₁	❏₂	❏₃	❏₄
CC02Q13	41) I read in my spare time.				
CC02Q14	42) I do my best work when I work with other students.	❏₁	❏₂	❏₃	❏₄
CC02Q15	43) Mathematics is one of my best subjects.	❏₁	❏₂	❏₃	❏₄
CC02Q16	44) I would like to be the best at something.				
CC02Q17	45) When I read, I sometimes get totally absorbed.	❏₁	❏₂	❏₃	❏₄
CC02Q18	46) I have always done well in mathematics.				
CC02Q19	47) I like to help other people do well in a group.	❏₁	❏₂	❏₃	❏₄
CC02Q20	48) I do well in tests in most school subjects.				
CC02Q21	49) Mathematics is important to me personally.	❏₁	❏₂	❏₃	❏₄
CC02Q22	50) It is helpful to put together everyone's ideas when working on a project.	❏₁	❏₂	❏₃	❏₄
CC02Q23	51) I get good marks in <test language>.	❏₁	❏₂	❏₃	❏₄
CC02Q24	52) I learn faster if I'm trying to do better than the others.	❏₁	❏₂	❏₃	❏₄

APPENDIX 3 **COMPUTER FAMILIARITY QUESTIONNAIRE**

Q 1   How often is there a computer available to you to use at these places?

(<Tick> one box on each line.)

		Almost every day	*A few times each week*	*Between once a week and once a month*	*Less than once a month*	*Never*
IT01Q01	a) At home.	$\square_1$	$\square_2$	$\square_3$	$\square_4$	$\square_5$
IT01Q02	b) At school.	$\square_1$	$\square_2$	$\square_3$	$\square_4$	$\square_5$
IT01Q03	c) In the library that you use.	$\square_1$	$\square_2$	$\square_3$	$\square_4$	$\square_5$
IT01Q04	d) At another place.	$\square_1$	$\square_2$	$\square_3$	$\square_4$	$\square_5$

Q 2   How comfortable:

(<Tick> one box on each line.)

		Very comfortable	*Comfortable*	*Somewhat comfortable*	*Not at all comfortable*
IT02Q01	a) are you with using a computer?	$\square_1$	$\square_2$	$\square_3$	$\square_4$
IT02Q02	b) are you with using a computer to write a paper?	$\square_1$	$\square_2$	$\square_3$	$\square_4$
IT02Q03	c) would you be taking a test on a computer?	$\square_1$	$\square_2$	$\square_3$	$\square_4$

IT03Q01   **Q 3   If you compare yourself with other 15-year-olds, how would you rate your ability to use a computer?**

Excellent	*Good*	*Fair*	*Poor*
$\square_1$	$\square_2$	$\square_3$	$\square_4$

Q 4   How often do you use a computer:

(<Tick> one box on each line.)

		Almost every day	*A few times each week*	*Between once a week and once a month*	*Less than once a month*	*Never*
IT04Q01	a) at home?	$\square_1$	$\square_2$	$\square_3$	$\square_4$	$\square_5$
IT04Q02	b) at school?	$\square_1$	$\square_2$	$\square_3$	$\square_4$	$\square_5$
IT04Q03	c) in the library that you use?	$\square_1$	$\square_2$	$\square_3$	$\square_4$	$\square_5$
IT04Q04	d) at another place?	$\square_1$	$\square_2$	$\square_3$	$\square_4$	$\square_5$

Q 5 How often do you use:
(<Tick> one box on each line.)

	Almost every day	A few times each week	Between once a week and once a month	Less than once a month	Never
IT05Q01 a) the Internet?	$\square_1$	$\square_2$	$\square_3$	$\square_4$	$\square_5$
IT05Q02 b) a computer for electronic communication (*e.g.* e-mail or "chat rooms")?	$\square_1$	$\square_2$	$\square_3$	$\square_4$	$\square_5$
IT05Q03 c) the computer to help you learn school material?	$\square_1$	$\square_2$	$\square_3$	$\square_4$	$\square_5$
IT05Q04 d) the computer for programming?	$\square_1$	$\square_2$	$\square_3$	$\square_4$	$\square_5$

Q 6 How often do you use each of the following kinds of computer software?
(<Tick> one box on each line.)

	Almost every day	A few times each week	Between once a week and once a month	Less than once a month	Never
IT06Q01 a) Games.	$\square_1$	$\square_2$	$\square_3$	$\square_4$	$\square_5$
IT06Q02 b) Word processing (e.g. Word ® or Word Perfect®).	$\square_1$	$\square_2$	$\square_3$	$\square_4$	$\square_5$
IT06Q03 c) Spreadsheets (e.g., Lotus 1 2 3 ® or Microsoft Excel®).	$\square_1$	$\square_2$	$\square_3$	$\square_4$	$\square_5$
IT06Q04 d) Drawing, painting or graphics.	$\square_1$	$\square_2$	$\square_3$	$\square_4$	$\square_5$
IT06Q05 e) Educational software.	$\square_1$	$\square_2$	$\square_3$	$\square_4$	$\square_5$

IT07Q01 **Q 7** It is very important to me to work with a computer.

Yes $\square_1$ No $\square_2$

IT08Q01 **Q 8** To play or work with a computer is really fun.

Yes $\square_1$ No $\square_2$

IT09Q01 **Q 9** I use a computer because I am very interested in this.

Yes $\square_1$ No $\square_2$

IT10Q01 **Q 10** I forget the time, when I am working with the computer.

Yes $\square_1$ No $\square_2$

APPENDIX 4 SCHOOL QUESTIONNAIRE

SC01Q01 **Q 1** **Which of the following best describes the community in which your school is located?**
(Please <tick> only one box.)

A <village, hamlet or rural area> (fewer than 3 000 people). ❏₁

A <small town> (3 000 to about 15 000 people). ❏₂

A <town> (15 000 to about 100 000 people). ❏₃

A <city> (100 000 to about 1 000 000 people). ❏₄

Close to the centre of a <city> with over 1 000 000 people. ❏₅

Elsewhere in a <city> with over 1 000 000 people. ❏₆

Q 2 **As at <March 31, 2000>, what was the total school enrolment (number of students)?**
<reminder note>
(Please write in a number on each row. Write 0 (zero) if there is none.)

SC02Q01 a) Number of boys: _____

SC02Q02 b) Number of girls: _____

SC03Q01 **Q 3** **Is your school a <public> or a <private> school?**
(Please <tick> only one box.)

A <public> school ❏₁
(This is a school managed directly or indirectly by a public education authority, government agency, or governing board appointed by government or elected by public franchise.)

A <private> school ❏₂
(This is a school managed directly or indirectly by a non-government organisation; e.g., a church, trade union, businesses, other private institutions.)

Q 4 **About what percentage of your total funding for a typical school year comes from the following sources?**
<reminder note>
(Please write in a number on each row. Write 0 (zero) if there is none.)

Percentage

SC04Q01 a) Government (includes departments, local, regional, state and national). _____ %

SC04Q02 b) Student fees or school charges paid by parents. _____ %

		Percentage
SC04Q03	c) Benefactors, donations, bequests, sponsorships, parent fund raising.	_____ %
SC04Q04	d) Other.	_____ %
	Total	*100 %*

Q 5 Are the following <grade levels> found in your school?

(Please <tick> one box on each row.)

		Yes	*No*
SC05Q01	a) <Grade 1>	❏₁	❏₂
SC05Q02	b) <Grade 2>	❏₁	❏₂
SC05Q03	c) <Grade 3>	❏₁	❏₂
SC05Q04	d) <Grade 4>	❏₁	❏₂
SC05Q05	e) <Grade 5>	❏₁	❏₂
SC05Q06	f) <Grade 6>	❏₁	❏₂
SC05Q07	g) <Grade 7>	❏₁	❏₂
SC05Q08	h) <Grade 8>	❏₁	❏₂
SC05Q09	i) <Grade 9>	❏₁	❏₂
SC05Q10	j) <Grade 10>	❏₁	❏₂
SC05Q11	k) <Grade 11>	❏₁	❏₂
SC05Q12	l) <Grade 12>	❏₁	❏₂
SC05Q13	m) <Grade 13>	❏₁	❏₂
SC05Q14	n) <Ungraded school>	❏₁	❏₂

Q 6 The following question refers to different aspects of instructional time for 15-year-old students in your school.

<If 15-year-olds are in different programmes or <grades>, choose the one where most of the 15-year-olds are located.>

(Please write in a number on each row. Write 0 (zero) if there is none.)

SC06Q01	a) How many instructional <u>weeks</u> are there in the school <u>year</u>?	_____ weeks
SC06Q02	b) How many <class periods> are there in the school <u>week</u>?	_____ <class periods>
SC06Q03	c) How many instructional <u>minutes</u> are there in the average single <class period>?	_____ minutes

Q 7 **How often are the following factors considered when students are admitted to your school?**

(Please <tick> one box on each row.)

		Never	*Sometimes*	*Always*
SC07Q01	a) Residence in a particular area.	❏₁	❏₂	❏₃
SC07Q02	b) Student's record of academic performance (including placement tests).	❏₁	❏₂	❏₃
SC07Q03	c) Recommendation of feeder schools.	❏₁	❏₂	❏₃
SC07Q04	d) Parents' endorsement of the instructional or religious philosophy of the school.	❏₁	❏₂	❏₃
SC07Q05	e) Whether the student requires or is interested in a special programme.	❏₁	❏₂	❏₃
SC07Q06	f) Preference given to family members of current or former students.	❏₁	❏₂	❏₃
SC07Q07	g) Other.	❏₁	❏₂	❏₃

Q 8 **In your school, what percentage of _15-year-old students_ is studying each programme?**
<Reminder note>
(Please write in a number on each row. Write 0 (zero) if there is none.)

		Percentage
SC08Q01	a) <ISCED 2A>	_____ %
SC08Q02	b) <ISCED 2B>	_____ %
SC08Q03	c) <ISCED 2C>	_____ %
SC08Q04	d) <ISCED 3A>	_____ %
SC08Q05	e) <ISCED 3B>	_____ %
SC08Q06	f) <ISCED 3C>	_____ %
	Total	*100 %*

Q 9 **In your school, how important is each of the following factors in determining the study programme of <15-year-old students>?**

(Please <tick> one box on each row.)

		Not important	*Important*	*Very important*
SC09Q01	a) Students' choice.	❏₁	❏₂	❏₃
SC09Q02	b) Students' previous academic record.	❏₁	❏₂	❏₃
SC09Q03	c) A placement examination.	❏₁	❏₂	❏₃
SC09Q04	d) Teachers' recommendation.	❏₁	❏₂	❏₃
SC09Q05	e) Parents' or guardians' request.	❏₁	❏₂	❏₃

Q 10 In your school, how likely is it that a <15-year-old student> would be transferred to another school because of:

(Please <tick> one box on each row.)

If students are never transferred, go to Q 11.

		Not likely	Likely	Very likely
SC10Q01	a) low academic achievement.	$\square_1$	$\square_2$	$\square_3$
SC10Q02	b) high academic achievement.	$\square_1$	$\square_2$	$\square_3$
SC10Q03	c) behavioural problems.	$\square_1$	$\square_2$	$\square_3$
SC10Q04	d) special learning needs.	$\square_1$	$\square_2$	$\square_3$
SC10Q05	e) parents' or guardians' request.	$\square_1$	$\square_2$	$\square_3$
SC10Q06	f) other.	$\square_1$	$\square_2$	$\square_3$

Q 11 In your school, how much is the learning of <15-year-old students> hindered by:

(Please <tick> one box on each row.)

		Not at all	Very little	To some extent	A lot
SC11Q01	a) poor condition of buildings?	$\square_1$	$\square_2$	$\square_3$	$\square_4$
SC11Q02	b) poor heating, cooling and/or lighting systems?	$\square_1$	$\square_2$	$\square_3$	$\square_4$
SC11Q03	c) lack of instructional space (e.g., classrooms)?	$\square_1$	$\square_2$	$\square_3$	$\square_4$
SC11Q04	d) lack of instructional material (e.g., textbooks)?	$\square_1$	$\square_2$	$\square_3$	$\square_4$
SC11Q05	e) not enough computers for instruction?	$\square_1$	$\square_2$	$\square_3$	$\square_4$
SC11Q06	f) lack of instructional materials in the library?	$\square_1$	$\square_2$	$\square_3$	$\square_4$
SC11Q07	g) lack of multi-media resources for instruction?	$\square_1$	$\square_2$	$\square_3$	$\square_4$
SC11Q08	h) inadequate science laboratory equipment?	$\square_1$	$\square_2$	$\square_3$	$\square_4$
SC11Q09	i) inadequate facilities for the fine arts?	$\square_1$	$\square_2$	$\square_3$	$\square_4$

Q 12 For <15-year-old students>, does your school provide the following resources?

(Please <tick> one box on each row.)

		Yes	No
SC12Q01	a) Extra courses on academic subjects for gifted students.	$\square_1$	$\square_2$
SC12Q02	b) Special training in <test language> for low achievers.	$\square_1$	$\square_2$
SC12Q03	c) Special courses in study skills for low achievers.	$\square_1$	$\square_2$
SC12Q04	d) Special tutoring by staff members.	$\square_1$	$\square_2$
SC12Q05	e) Room(s) where the students can do their homework with staff help.	$\square_1$	$\square_2$

Q 13   In your school, about how many computers are:

<reminder note>

(Please write in a number on each row. Write 0 (zero) if there is none.)

		Number
SC13Q01	a) in the school altogether?	_____
SC13Q02	b) available to 15-year-old students?	_____
SC13Q03	c) available only to teachers?	_____
SC13Q04	d) available only to administrative staff?	_____
SC13Q05	e) connected to the Internet/World Wide Web?	_____
SC13Q06	f) connected to a local area network (LAN, Intranet)?	_____

Q 14   In your school, how many full-time and part-time teachers:

A full-time teacher is employed at least 90% of the time as a classroom teacher. All other teachers should be considered part-time.

Note that categories b) to i) are not mutually exclusive, so the total item a) may be less than the sum of items b) to i).

<reminder note>

(Please write in a number in each space provided. Write 0 (zero) if there is none.)

		Full-time	*Part-time*
SC14Q01 SC14Q02	a) are there in TOTAL?	_____	_____
SC14Q03 SC14Q04	b) have a <ISCED5A> qualification in <pedagogy>?	_____	_____
SC14Q05 SC14Q06	c) are fully certified as teachers by <the appropriate authority>?	_____	_____
SC14Q07 SC14Q08	d) are <test language> teachers?	_____	_____
SC14Q09 SC14Q10	e) have a <ISCED5A> qualification <with a major> in <test language>?	_____	_____
SC14Q11 SC14Q12	f) are <mathematics> teachers?	_____	_____
SC14Q13 SC14Q14	g) have a <ISCED5A> qualification <with a major> in <mathematics>?	_____	_____
SC14Q15 SC14Q16	h) are <science> teachers?	_____	_____
SC14Q17 SC14Q18	i) have a <ISCED5A> qualification <with a major> in <science>?	_____	_____

SC15Q01 **Q 15** During the last three months, what percentage of teaching staff in your school have attended a programme of professional development?

<reminder note>

> Professional development is a formal programme designed to enhance teaching skills or pedagogical practices. It may or may not lead to a recognised qualification. The total length of the programme must last for at least one day and have a focus on teaching and education.

_____ %

Q 16 Generally, in your school how often are <15-year-old students> assessed using:

(Please <tick> one box in each row.)

	Never	Yearly	2 times a year	3 times a year	4 or more times a year
SC16Q01 a) standardised tests?	$\square_1$	$\square_2$	$\square_3$	$\square_4$	$\square_5$
SC16Q02 b) teacher-developed tests?	$\square_1$	$\square_2$	$\square_3$	$\square_4$	$\square_5$
SC16Q03 c) teachers' judgmental ratings?	$\square_1$	$\square_2$	$\square_3$	$\square_4$	$\square_5$
SC16Q04 d) student <portfolios>?	$\square_1$	$\square_2$	$\square_3$	$\square_4$	$\square_5$
SC16Q05 e) student assignments/projects/homework?	$\square_1$	$\square_2$	$\square_3$	$\square_4$	$\square_5$

Q 17 In your school, about how often is information on the performance of <15-year-old students> formally communicated to:

(Please <tick> one box on each row.)

	Never	Yearly	2 times a year	3 times a year	4 or more times a year
SC17Q01 a) parents?	$\square_1$	$\square_2$	$\square_3$	$\square_4$	$\square_5$
SC17Q02 b) school <principal>?	$\square_1$	$\square_2$	$\square_3$	$\square_4$	$\square_5$
SC17Q03 c) <district/government administrators>?	$\square_1$	$\square_2$	$\square_3$	$\square_4$	$\square_5$

Q 18 In your school, are assessments of <15-year-old students> used to:

(Please <tick> one box on each row.)

	Yes	No
SC18Q01 a) inform parents about their child's progress?	$\square_1$	$\square_2$
SC18Q02 b) make decisions about retention or promotion?	$\square_1$	$\square_2$
SC18Q03 c) group students for instructional purposes?	$\square_1$	$\square_2$
SC18Q04 d) compare the school to <district or national> performance?	$\square_1$	$\square_2$
SC18Q05 e) monitor the school's progress from year to year?	$\square_1$	$\square_2$
SC18Q06 f) make judgments about teachers' effectiveness?	$\square_1$	$\square_2$

Q 19 In your school, is the learning of <15-year-old students> hindered by:

(Please <tick> one box on each row.)

		Not at all	*Very little*	*To some extent*	*A lot*
SC19Q01	a) low expectations of teachers?	☐₁	☐₂	☐₃	☐₄
SC19Q02	b) student absenteeism?	☐₁	☐₂	☐₃	☐₄
SC19Q03	c) poor student-teacher relations?	☐₁	☐₂	☐₃	☐₄
SC19Q04	d) teacher turnover?	☐₁	☐₂	☐₃	☐₄
SC19Q05	e) lack of parental support for student learning at home?	☐₁	☐₂	☐₃	☐₄
SC19Q06	f) disruption of classes by students?	☐₁	☐₂	☐₃	☐₄
SC19Q07	g) teachers not meeting individual students' needs?	☐₁	☐₂	☐₃	☐₄
SC19Q08	h) teacher absenteeism?				
SC19Q09	i) students skipping classes?	☐₁	☐₂	☐₃	☐₄
SC19Q10	j) students lacking respect for teachers?	☐₁	☐₂	☐₃	☐₄
SC19Q11	k) staff resisting change?	☐₁	☐₂	☐₃	☐₄
SC19Q12	l) not enough instructional time?	☐₁	☐₂	☐₃	☐₄
SC19Q13	m) the use of alcohol or illegal drugs?	☐₁	☐₂	☐₃	☐₄
SC19Q14	n) teachers being too strict with students?	☐₁	☐₂	☐₃	☐₄
SC19Q15	o) students intimidating or bullying other students?	☐₁	☐₂	☐₃	☐₄
SC19Q16	p) students not being encouraged to achieve their full potential?	☐₁	☐₂	☐₃	☐₄
SC19Q17	q) students coming from poor home environments?	☐₁	☐₂	☐₃	☐₄

Q 20 **Think about the teachers in your school. How much do you agree or disagree with the following statements?**

(Please <tick> one box on each row.)

		Strongly agree	*Disagree*	*Agreee*	*Strongly Disagree*
SC20Q01	a) The morale of teachers in this school is high.	☐₁	☐₂	☐₃	☐₄
SC20Q02	b) Teachers work with enthusiasm.	☐₁	☐₂	☐₃	☐₄
SC20Q03	c) Teachers take pride in this school.	☐₁	☐₂	☐₃	☐₄
SC20Q04	d) Teachers value academic achievement.	☐₁	☐₂	☐₃	☐₄

Q 21 **In your school, is the learning of <15-year-old students> hindered by:**

(Please <tick> one box on each row.)

		Not at all	*A little*	*Somewhat*	*A lot*
SC21Q01	a) a shortage/inadequacy of teachers?	❏₁	❏₂	❏₃	❏₄
SC21Q02	b) a shortage/inadequacy of <test language> teachers?	❏₁	❏₂	❏₃	❏₄
SC21Q03	c) a shortage/inadequacy of <mathematics> teachers?	❏₁	❏₂	❏₃	❏₄
SC21Q04	d) a shortage/inadequacy of <science> teachers?	❏₁	❏₂	❏₃	❏₄
SC21Q05	e) a shortage/inadequacy of support personnel for classroom teachers?	❏₁	❏₂	❏₃	❏₄

Q 22 **In your school, who has the main responsibility for:**

(Please <tick> as many boxes as appropriate on each row.)

		Not a school responsibility	*Appointed or elected board*	*Principal*	*Department head*	*Teachers*
SC22Q01	a) hiring teachers?	❏₁	❏₂	❏₃	❏₄	❏₅
SC22Q02	b) firing teachers?	❏₁	❏₂	❏₃	❏₄	❏₅
SC22Q03	c) establishing teachers' starting salaries?	❏₁	❏₂	❏₃	❏₄	❏₅
SC22Q04	d) Determining teachers' salary increases?	❏₁	❏₂	❏₃	❏₄	❏₅
SC22Q05	e) formulating the school budget?	❏₁	❏₂	❏₃	❏₄	❏₅
SC22Q06	f) deciding on budget allocations within the school?	❏₁	❏₂	❏₃	❏₄	❏₅
SC22Q07	g) establishing student disciplinary policies?	❏₁	❏₂	❏₃	❏₄	❏₅
SC22Q08	h) establishing student assessment policies?	❏₁	❏₂	❏₃	❏₄	❏₅
SC22Q09	i) approving students for admittance to school?	❏₁	❏₂	❏₃	❏₄	❏₅
SC22Q10	j) choosing which textbooks are used?	❏₁	❏₂	❏₃	❏₄	❏₅
SC22Q11	k) determining course content?	❏₁	❏₂	❏₃	❏₄	❏₅
SC22Q12	l) deciding which courses are offered?	❏₁	❏₂	❏₃	❏₄	❏₅

APPENDIX 5 **STUDENT QUESTIONNAIRE DATA FILE CODEBOOK**

COUNTRY	Country three-digit code	(A3)	2-4
SCHOOLID	School ID (unique)	(A5)	5-9
STIDSTD	Student ID	(A5)	10-14
SUBNATIO	Subnational entities	(A2)	16-17

ST01Q01 Birth Day - Q1 Day (A2) 19-20
97 N/A
99 Mis

ST01Q02 Birth Month - Q1 Month (A2) 21-22
97 N/A
99 Mis

ST01Q03 Birth Year - Q1 Year (A4) 23-26
9997 N/A
9999 Mis

ST02Q01 Grade - Q2 (F2.0) 27-28
97 N/A
99 Mis

ST03Q01 Sex - Q3 (F1.0) 29-29
1 Female
2 Male
7 N/A
8 M/R
9 Mis

ST04Q01 Mother - Q4a (F1.0) 30-30
1 Yes
2 No
7 N/A
8 M/R
9 Mis

ST04Q02 Female Guardian - Q4b (F1.0) 31-31
1 Yes
2 No
7 N/A
8 M/R
9 Mis

ST04Q03 Father - Q4c (F1.0) 32-32
1 Yes
2 No
7 N/A
8 M/R
9 Mis

ST04Q04 Male Guardian - Q4d (F1.0) 33-33
1 Yes
2 No
7 N/A
8 M/R
9 Mis

ST04Q05 Brothers - Q4e (F1.0) 34-34
1 Yes
2 No
7 N/A
8 M/R
9 Mis

ST04Q06 Sisters - Q4f (F1.0) 35-35
1 Yes
2 No
7 N/A
8 M/R
9 Mis

ST04Q07 Grandparents - Q4g (F1.0) 36-36
1 Yes
2 No
7 N/A
8 M/R
9 Mis

ST04Q08 Others - Q4h (F1.0) 37-37
1 Yes
2 No
7 N/A
8 M/R
9 Mis

ST05Q01	*Older - Q5a*	(F1.0) 38-38
	1	None
	2	One
	3	Two
	4	Three
	5	Four or more
	7	N/A
	8	M/R
	9	Mis

ST05Q02	*Younger - Q5b*	(F1.0) 39-39
	1	None
	2	One
	3	Two
	4	Three
	5	Four or more
	7	N/A
	8	M/R
	9	Mis

ST05Q03	*Same age - Q5c*	(F1.0) 40-40
	1	None
	2	One
	3	Two
	4	Three
	5	Four or more
	7	N/A
	8	M/R
	9	Mis

ST06Q01	*Mother currently doing - Q6*	(F1.0) 41-41
	1	Working full-time
	2	Working part-time
	3	Looking for job
	4	Other
	7	N/A
	8	M/R
	9	Mis

ST07Q01	*Father currently doing - Q7*	(F1.0) 42-42
	1	Working full-time
	2	Working part-time
	3	Looking for job
	4	Other
	7	N/A
	8	M/R
	9	Mis

ST09Q01	*Mother's main job - Q8&9*	(A4) 43-46
	9997	N/A
	9999	MIS

ST11Q01	*Father's main job - Q10&11*	(A4) 47-50
	9997	N/A
	9999	MIS

ST12Q01	*Mother's secondary educ - Q12*	(F1.0) 51-51
	1	Didn't go to school
	2	Completed ISCED 1
	3	Completed ISCED 2
	4	Completed ISCED 3B 3C
	5	Completed ISCED 3A
	7	N/A
	8	M/R
	9	Mis

ST13Q01	*Father's secondary educ -Q13*	(F1.0) 52-52
	1	Didn't go to school
	2	Completed ISCED 1
	3	Completed ISCED 2
	4	Completed ISCED 3B 3C
	5	Completed ISCED 3A
	7	N/A
	8	M/R
	9	Mis

ST14Q01	*Mother's tertiary educ -Q14*	(F1.0) 53-53
	1	Yes
	2	No
	7	N/A
	8	M/R
	9	Mis

ST15Q01	*Father's tertiary educ - Q15*	(F1.0) 54-54
	1	Yes
	2	No
	7	N/A
	8	M/R
	9	Mis

ST16Q01	*Country of birth, self - Q16a*	(F1.0) 55-55
	1	<Country of Test>
	2	Other
	7	N/A
	8	M/R
	9	Mis

ST16Q02	*Country of birth, Mother - Q16b*	(F1.0) 56-56
	1	<Country of Test>
	2	Other
	7	N/A
	8	M/R
	9	Mis

ST16Q03	*Country of birth, Father - Q16c*	(F1.0) 57-57
	1	<Country of Test>
	2	Other
	7	N/A
	8	M/R
	9	Mis

ST17Q01	*Language at home - Q17*	(F1.0) 58-58
	1	<Test language>
	2	<Other official languages>
	3	<National Dialects>
	4	<Other Languages>
	7	N/A
	8	M/R
	9	Mis

ST18Q01	*Movies - Q18a*	(F1.0) 59-59
	1	Never
	2	1 or 2 times a year
	3	3 or 4 times a year
	4	More 4 times a year
	7	N/A
	8	M/R
	9	Mis

ST18Q02	*Art gallery - Q18b*	(F1.0) 60-60
	1	Never
	2	1 or 2 times a year
	3	3 or 4 times a year
	4	More 4 times a year
	7	N/A
	8	M/R
	9	Mis

ST18Q03	*Pop Music - Q18c*	(F1.0) 61-61
	1	Never
	2	1 or 2 times a year
	3	3 or 4 times a year
	4	More 4 times a year
	7	N/A
	8	M/R
	9	Mis

ST18Q04	*Opera - Q18d*	(F1.0) 62-62
	1	Never
	2	1 or 2 times a year
	3	3 or 4 times a year
	4	More 4 times a year
	7	N/A
	8	M/R
	9	Mis

ST18Q05	*Theatre - Q18e*	(F1.0) 63-63
	1	Never
	2	1 or 2 times a year
	3	3 or 4 times a year
	4	More 4 times a year
	7	N/A
	8	M/R
	9	Mis

ST18Q06	*Sport - Q18f*	(F1.0) 64-64
	1	Never
	2	1 or 2 times a year
	3	3 or 4 times a year
	4	More 4 times a year
	7	N/A
	8	M/R
	9	Mis

ST19Q01 *Discuss politics - Q19a*   (F1.0) 65-65

1	Never
2	Few times/year
3	Once a month
4	Several times/month
5	Several times/week
7	N/A
8	M/R
9	Mis

ST19Q02 *Discuss books - Q19b*   (F1.0) 66-66

1	Never
2	Few times/year
3	Once a month
4	Several times/month
5	Several times/week
7	N/A
8	M/R
9	Mis

ST19Q03 *Listen classics - Q19c*   (F1.0) 67-67

1	Never
2	Few times/year
3	Once a month
4	Several times/month
5	Several times/week
7	N/A
8	M/R
9	Mis

ST19Q04 *Discuss school issues - Q19d*   (F1.0) 68-68

1	Never
2	Few times/year
3	Once a month
4	Several times/month
5	Several times/week
7	N/A
8	M/R
9	Mis

ST19Q05 *Eat <main meal> - Q19e* (F1.0) 69-69

1	Never
2	Few times/year
3	Once a month
4	Several times/month
5	Several times/week
7	N/A
8	M/R
9	Mis

ST19Q06 *Just talking - Q19f*   (F1.0)   70-70

1	Never
2	Few times/year
3	Once a month
4	Several times/month
5	Several times/week
7	N/A
8	M/R
9	Mis

ST20Q01 *Mother - Q20a*   (F1.0) 71-71

1	Never
2	Few times/year
3	Once a month
4	Several times/month
5	Several times/week
7	N/A
8	M/R
9	Mis

ST20Q02 *Father - Q20b*   (F1.0) 72-72

1	Never
2	Few times/year
3	Once a month
4	Several times/month
5	Several times/week
7	N/A
8	M/R
9	Mis

ST20Q03 *Siblings - Q20c*   (F1.0) 73-73
1   Never
2   Few times/year
3   Once a month
4   Several times/month
5   Several times/week
7   N/A
8   M/R
9   Mis

ST20Q04 *Grandparents - Q20d*   (F1.0) 74-74
1   Never
2   Few times/year
3   Once a month
4   Several times/month
5   Several times/week
7   N/A
8   M/R
9   Mis

ST20Q05 *Other Relations - Q20e*   (F1.0) 75-75
1   Never
2   Few times/year
3   Once a month
4   Several times/month
5   Several times/week
7   N/A
8   M/R
9   Mis

ST20Q06 *Parents' friends - Q20f* (F1.0) 76-76
1   Never
2   Few times/year
3   Once a month
4   Several times/month
5   Several times/week
7   N/A
8   M/R
9   Mis

ST21Q01 *Dishwasher - Q21a*   (F1.0) 77-77
1   Yes
2   No
7   N/A
8   M/R
9   Mis

ST21Q02 *Own room - Q21b*   (F1.0) 78-78
1   Yes
2   No
7   N/A
8   M/R
9   Mis

ST21Q03 *Educat software - Q21c*   (F1.0) 79-79
1   Yes
2   No
7   N/A
8   M/R
9   Mis

ST21Q04 *Internet - Q21d*   (F1.0) 80-80
1   Yes
2   No
7   N/A
8   M/R
9   Mis

ST21Q05 *Dictionary - Q21e*   (F1.0) 81-81
1   Yes
2   No
7   N/A
8   M/R
9   Mis

ST21Q06 *Study place - Q21f*   (F1.0) 82-82
1   Yes
2   No
7   N/A
8   M/R
9   Mis

ST21Q07	Desk - Q21g	(F1.0) 83-83
1	Yes	
2	No	
7	N/A	
8	M/R	
9	Mis	

ST21Q08	Text books - Q21h	(F1.0) 84-84
1	Yes	
2	No	
7	N/A	
8	M/R	
9	Mis	

ST21Q09	Classic literature - Q21i	(F1.0) 85-85
1	Yes	
2	No	
7	N/A	
8	M/R	
9	Mis	

ST21Q10	Poetry - Q21j	(F1.0) 86-86
1	Yes	
2	No	
7	N/A	
8	M/R	
9	Mis	

ST21Q11	Art works - Q21k	(F1.0) 87-87
1	Yes	
2	No	
7	N/A	
8	M/R	
9	Mis	

ST22Q01	Phone - Q22a	(F1.0) 88-88
1	None	
2	One	
3	Two	
4	3 or more	
7	N/A	
8	M/R	
9	Mis	

ST22Q02	Television - Q22b	(F1.0) 89-89
1	None	
2	One	
3	Two	
4	3 or more	
7	N/A	
8	M/R	
9	Mis	

ST22Q03	Calculator - Q22c	(F1.0) 90-90
1	None	
2	One	
3	Two	
4	3 or more	
7	N/A	
8	M/R	
9	Mis	

ST22Q04	Computer - Q22d	(F1.0) 91-91
1	None	
2	One	
3	Two	
4	3 or more	
7	N/A	
8	M/R	
9	Mis	

ST22Q05	Musical instruments - Q22e	(F1.0) 92-92
1	None	
2	One	
3	Two	
4	3 or more	
7	N/A	
8	M/R	
9	Mis	

ST22Q06	Car - Q22f	(F1.0) 93-93
1	None	
2	One	
3	Two	
4	3 or more	
7	N/A	
8	M/R	
9	Mis	

ST22Q07	*Bathroom - Q22g*	(F1.0)	94-94
1	None		
2	One		
3	Two		
4	3 or more		
7	N/A		
8	M/R		
9	Mis		

ST23Q01	*<Extension> - Q23a*	(F1.0)	95-95
1	Never		
2	Some		
3	Regular		
7	N/A		
8	M/R		
9	Mis		

ST23Q02	*<Remedial> in <test lang> - Q23b*	(F1.0)	96-96
1	Never		
2	Some		
3	Regular		
7	N/A		
8	M/R		
9	Mis		

ST23Q03	*<Remedial> in other subjects - Q23c*	(F1.0)	97-97
1	Never		
2	Some		
3	Regular		
7	N/A		
8	M/R		
9	Mis		

ST23Q04	*Skills training - Q23d*	(F1.0)	98-98
1	Never		
2	Some		
3	Regular		
7	N/A		
8	M/R		
9	Mis		

ST24Q01	*In <test language> - Q24a*	(F1.0)	99-99
1	Never		
2	Some		
3	Regular		
7	N/A		
8	M/R		
9	Mis		

ST24Q02	*In other subjects - Q24b*	(F1.0)	100-100
1	Never		
2	Some		
3	Regular		
7	N/A		
8	M/R		
9	Mis		

ST24Q03	*<Extension> - Q24c*	(F1.0)	101-101
1	Never		
2	Some		
3	Regular		
7	N/A		
8	M/R		
9	Mis		

ST24Q04	*<Remedial> in <test language> - Q24d*	(F1.0)	102-102
1	Never		
2	Some		
3	Regular		
7	N/A		
8	M/R		
9	Mis		

ST24Q05	*<Remedial> in other subjects - Q24e*	(F1.0)	103-103
1	Never		
2	Some		
3	Regular		
7	N/A		
8	M/R		
9	Mis		

ST24Q06 *Skills training - Q24f* (F1.0) 104-104
1   Never
2   Some
3   Regular
7   N/A
8   M/R
9   Mis

ST24Q07 *<Private tutoring> - Q24g* (F1.0) 105-105
1   Never
2   Some
3   Regular
7   N/A
8   M/R
9   Mis

ST25Q01 *School program - Q25* (F1.0) 106-106
1   <ISCED 2A>
2   <ISCED 2B>
3   <ISCED 2C>
4   <ISCED 3A>
5   <ISCED 3B>
6   <ISCED 3C>
7   N/A
8   M/R
9   Mis

ST26Q01 *Teachers wait long time - Q26a* (F1.0) 107-107
1   Never
2   Some lessons
3   Most lessons
4   Every lesson
7   N/A
8   M/R
9   Mis

ST26Q02 *Teachers want students to work - Q26b* (F1.0) 108-108
1   Never
2   Some lessons
3   Most lessons
4   Every lesson
7   N/A
8   M/R
9   Mis

ST26Q03 *Teachers tell students do better - Q26c* (F1.0) 109-109
1   Never
2   Some lessons
3   Most lessons
4   Every lesson
7   N/A
8   M/R
9   Mis

ST26Q04 *Teachers don't like - Q26d* (F1.0) 110-110
1   Never
2   Some lessons
3   Most lessons
4   Every lesson
7   N/A
8   M/R
9   Mis

ST26Q05 *Teachers show interest - Q26e* (F1.0) 111-111
1   Never
2   Some lessons
3   Most lessons
4   Every lesson
7   N/A
8   M/R
9   Mis

ST26Q06 *Teachers give opportunity - Q26f* (F1.0) 112-112
1   Never
2   Some lessons
3   Most lessons
4   Every lesson
7   N/A
8   M/R
9   Mis

ST26Q07 *Teachers help with work - Q26g* (F1.0) 113-113
1   Never
2   Some lessons
3   Most lessons
4   Every lesson
7   N/A
8   M/R
9   Mis

ST26Q08 *Teachers*
continue teaching - Q26h   (F1.0) 114-114
1   Never
2   Some lessons
3   Most lessons
4   Every lesson
7   N/A
8   M/R
9   Mis

ST26Q09 *Teachers do a lot to help- Q26i* (F1.0) 115-115
1   Never
2   Some lessons
3   Most lessons
4   Every lesson
7   N/A
8   M/R
9   Mis

ST26Q10 *Teachers help*
with learning - Q26j   (F1.0) 116-116
1   Never
2   Some lessons
3   Most lessons
4   Every lesson
7   N/A
8   M/R
9   Mis

ST26Q11 *Teachers check*
homework - Q26k   (F1.0) 117-117
1   Never
2   Some lessons
3   Most lessons
4   Every lesson
7   N/A
8   M/R
9   Mis

ST26Q12 *Students cannot*
work well - Q26l   (F1.0) 118-118
1   Never
2   Some lessons
3   Most lessons
4   Every lesson
7   N/A
8   M/R
9   Mis

ST26Q13 *Students don't listen - Q26m*   (F1.0) 119-119
1   Never
2   Some lessons
3   Most lessons
4   Every lesson
7   N/A
8   M/R
9   Mis

ST26Q14 *Students don't start - Q26n*   (F1.0) 120-120
1   Never
2   Some lessons
3   Most lessons
4   Every lesson
7   N/A
8   M/R
9   Mis

ST26Q15 *Students learn a lot - Q26o*   (F1.0) 121-121
1   Never
2   Some lessons
3   Most lessons
4   Every lesson
7   N/A
8   M/R
9   Mis

ST26Q16 *Noise & disorder - Q26p*   (F1.0) 122-122
1   Never
2   Some lessons
3   Most lessons
4   Every lesson
7   N/A
8   M/R
9   Mis

ST26Q17 *Doing nothing - Q26q*   (F1.0) 123-123
1   Never
2   Some lessons
3   Most lessons
4   Every lesson
7   N/A
8   M/R
9   Mis

ST27Q01 *Hours in*
<test language> - Q27a (F2.0) 124-125
97 N/A
99 Mis

ST27Q02 *Usual in*
<test language> - Q27aa (F1.0) 126-126
1 Yes
2 No
7 N/A
8 M/R
9 Mis

ST27Q03 *Hours in Mathematics - Q27b*
97 N/A
99 MIS

ST27Q04 *Usual in*
Mathematics - Q27bb (F1.0) 129-129
1 Yes
2 No
7 N/A
8 M/R
9 Mis

ST27Q05 *Hours in Science - Q27c* (F2.0) 130-131
97 N/A
99 MIS

ST27Q06 *Usual in Science - Q27cc* (F1.0) 132-132
1 Yes
2 No
7 N/A
8 M/R
9 Mis

ST28Q01 *Number of students in*
<test language> - Q28a (F2.0) 133-134
97 N/A
99 Mis

ST28Q02 *Number of students*
in Mathematics - Q28b (F2.0) 135-136
97 N/A
99 Mis

ST28Q03 *Number of students*
in Science - Q28c (F2.0) 137-138
97 N/A
99 Mis

ST29Q01 *Miss school - Q29a* (F1.0) 139-139
1 None
2 1 or 2
3 3 or 4
4 5 or more
7 N/A
8 M/R
9 Mis

ST29Q02 *<Skip> classes - Q29b* (F1.0) 140-140
1 None
2 1 or 2
3 3 or 4
4 5 or more
7 N/A
8 M/R
9 Mis

ST29Q03 *Late for school - Q29c* (F1.0) 141-141
1 None
2 1 or 2
3 3 or 4
4 5 or more
7 N/A
8 M/R
9 Mis

ST30Q01 *Well with teachers - Q30a* (F1.0) 142-142
1 Strongly disagree
2 Disagree
3 Agree
4 Strongly agree
7 N/A
8 M/R
9 Mis

ST30Q02 *Interested in students - Q30b* (F1.0) 143-143
1 Strongly disagree
2 Disagree
3 Agree
4 Strongly agree
7 N/A
8 M/R
9 Mis

ST30Q03 *Listen to me - Q30c*   (F1.0) 144-144
1   Strongly disagree
2   Disagree
3   Agree
4   Strongly agree
7   N/A
8   M/R
9   Mis

ST30Q04 *Give extra help - Q30d*   (F1.0) 145-145
1   Strongly disagree
2   Disagree
3   Agree
4   Strongly agree
7   N/A
8   M/R
9   Mis

ST30Q05 *Treat me fairly - Q30e*   (F1.0) 146-146
1   Strongly disagree
2   Disagree
3   Agree
4   Strongly agree
7   N/A
8   M/R
9   Mis

ST31Q01 *Feel an outsider - Q31a*   (F1.0) 147-147
1   Strongly disagree
2   Disagree
3   Agree
4   Strongly agree
7   N/A
8   M/R
9   Mis

ST31Q02 *Make friends - Q31b*   (F1.0) 148-148
1   Strongly disagree
2   Disagree
3   Agree
4   Strongly agree
7   N/A
8   M/R
9   Mis

ST31Q03 *Feel I belong - Q31c*   (F1.0) 149-149
1   Strongly disagree
2   Disagree
3   Agree
4   Strongly agree
7   N/A
8   M/R
9   Mis

ST31Q04 *Feel awkward - Q31d*   (F1.0) 150-150
1   Strongly disagree
2   Disagree
3   Agree
4   Strongly agree
7   N/A
8   M/R
9   Mis

ST31Q05 *Seem to like me - Q31e*   (F1.0) 151-151
1   Strongly disagree
2   Disagree
3   Agree
4   Strongly agree
7   N/A
8   M/R
9   Mis

ST31Q06 *Feel lonely - Q31f*   (F1.0) 152-152
1   Strongly disagree
2   Disagree
3   Agree
4   Strongly agree
7   N/A
8   M/R
9   Mis

ST31Q07 *Don't want to be - Q31g*   (F1.0) 153-153
1   Strongly disagree
2   Disagree
3   Agree
4   Strongly agree
7   N/A
8   M/R
9   Mis

ST31Q08	*Feel Bored - Q31h*	(F1.0)	154-154
	1	Strongly disagree	
	2	Disagree	
	3	Agree	
	4	Strongly agree	
	7	N/A	
	8	M/R	
	9	Mis	
ST32Q01	*I complete on time - Q32a*	(F1.0)	155-155
	1	Never	
	2	Smtime	
	3	Mostly	
	4	Always	
	7	N/A	
	8	M/R	
	9	Mis	
ST32Q02	*I do watching TV - Q32b*	(F1.0)	156-156
	1	Never	
	2	Smtime	
	3	Mostly	
	4	Always	
	7	N/A	
	8	M/R	
	9	Mis	
ST32Q03	*Teachers grade - Q32c*	(F1.0)	157-157
	1	Never	
	2	Smtime	
	3	Mostly	
	4	Always	
	7	N/A	
	8	M/R	
	9	Mis	
ST32Q04	*I finish at school - Q32d*	(F1.0)	158-158
	1	Never	
	2	Smtime	
	3	Mostly	
	4	Always	
	7	N/A	
	8	M/R	
	9	Mis	

ST32Q05	*Teachers comment on - Q32e*	(F1.0)	159-159
	1	Never	
	2	Smtime	
	3	Mostly	
	4	Always	
	7	N/A	
	8	M/R	
	9	Mis	
ST32Q06	*Is interesting - Q32f*	(F1.0)	160-160
	1	Never	
	2	Smtime	
	3	Mostly	
	4	Always	
	7	N/A	
	8	M/R	
	9	Mis	
ST32Q07	*Is counted in <mark> - Q32g*	(F1.0)	161-161
	1	Never	
	2	Smtime	
	3	Mostly	
	4	Always	
	7	N/A	
	8	M/R	
	9	Mis	
ST33Q01	*Homework <test language> - Q33a*	(F1.0)	162-162
	1	No time	
	2	< 1 h/week	
	3	1 to 3 h/week	
	4	> 3 h/week	
	7	N/A	
	8	M/R	
	9	Mis	
ST33Q02	*Homework <maths> - Q33b*	(F1.0)	163-163
	1	No time	
	2	< 1 h/week	
	3	1 to 3 h/week	
	4	> 3 h/week	
	7	N/A	
	8	M/R	
	9	Mis	

ST33Q03 *Homework
<science> - Q33c* (F1.0) 164-164
1 No time
2 < 1 h/week
3 1 to 3 h/week
4 > 3 h/week
7 N/A
8 M/R
9 Mis

ST34Q01 *Read each day - Q34* (F1.0) 165-165
1 Don't read
2 30 min or less
3 31- 60 min
4 1-2 hours
5 More than 2 hours
7 N/A
8 M/R
9 Mis

ST35Q01 *Only if I have to - Q35a* (F1.0) 166-166
1 Strongly disagree
2 Disagree
3 Agree
4 Strongly agree
7 N/A
8 M/R
9 Mis

ST35Q02 *Favourite hobby - Q35b* (F1.0) 167-167
1 Strongly disagree
2 Disagree
3 Agree
4 Strongly agree
7 N/A
8 M/R
9 Mis

ST35Q03 *Talking about books - Q35c* (F1.0) 168-168
1 Strongly disagree
2 Disagree
3 Agree
4 Strongly agree
7 N/A
8 M/R
9 Mis

ST35Q04 *Hard to finish - Q35d* (F1.0) 169-169
1 Strongly disagree
2 Disagree
3 Agree
4 Strongly agree
7 N/A
8 M/R
9 Mis

ST35Q05 *Feel happy - Q35e* (F1.0) 170-170
1 Strongly disagree
2 Disagree
3 Agree
4 Strongly agree
7 N/A
8 M/R
9 Mis

ST35Q06 *Waste of time - Q35f* (F1.0) 171-171
1 Strongly disagree
2 Disagree
3 Agree
4 Strongly agree
7 N/A
8 M/R
9 Mis

ST35Q07 *Enjoy library - Q35g* (F1.0) 172-172
1 Strongly disagree
2 Disagree
3 Agree
4 Strongly agree
7 N/A
8 M/R
9 Mis

ST35Q08 *For information - Q35h* (F1.0) 173-173
1 Strongly disagree
2 Disagree
3 Agree
4 Strongly agree
7 N/A
8 M/R
9 Mis

ST35Q09 *Few minutes only - Q35i* (F1.0) 174-174

1	Strongly disagree
2	Disagree
3	Agree
4	Strongly agree
7	N/A
8	M/R
9	Mis

ST36Q01 *Magazines - Q36a* (F1.0) 175-175

1	Never
2	Few times/year
3	Once/month
4	Several times/month
5	Several times/week
7	N/A
8	M/R
9	Mis

ST36Q02 *Comics - Q36b* (F1.0) 176-176

1	Never
2	Few times/year
3	Once/month
4	Several times/month
5	Several times/week
7	N/A
8	M/R
9	Mis

ST36Q03 *Fictions - Q36c* (F1.0) 177-177

1	Never
2	Few times/year
3	Once/month
4	Several times/month
5	Several times/week
7	N/A
8	M/R
9	Mis

ST36Q04 *Non-fiction - Q36d* (F1.0) 178-178

1	Never
2	Few times/year
3	Once/month
4	Several times/month
5	Several times/week
7	N/A
8	M/R
9	Mis

ST36Q05 *E-mail & Web - Q36e* (F1.0) 179-179

1	Never
2	Few times/year
3	Once/month
4	Several times/month
5	Several times/week
7	N/A
8	M/R
9	Mis

ST36Q06 *Newspapers - Q36f* (F1.0) 180-180

1	Never
2	Few times/year
3	Once/month
4	Several times/month
5	Several times/week
7	N/A
8	M/R
9	Mis

ST37Q01 *How many books at home - Q37* (F2.0) 181-182

1	None
2	1-10
3	11-50
4	51-100
5	101-250
6	251-500
7	More than 500
97	N/A
98	M/R
99	Mis

ST38Q01	*Borrow books - Q38*	(F1.0)	183-183

1 Never
2 Few times/year
3 Once a month
4 Several times/month
7 N/A
8 M/R
9 Mis

ST39Q01	*How often use school library - Q39a*	(F1.0)	184-184

1 Never
2 Few times/year
3 Once/month
4 Several times/month
5 Several times/week
7 N/A
8 M/R
9 Mis

ST39Q02	*How often use computers - Q39b*	(F1.0)	185-185

1 Never
2 Few times/year
3 Once/month
4 Several times/month
5 Several times/week
7 N/A
8 M/R
9 Mis

ST39Q03	*How often use calculators - Q39c*	(F1.0)	186-186

1 Never
2 Few times/year
3 Once/month
4 Several times/month
5 Several times/week
7 N/A
8 M/R
9 Mis

ST39Q04	*How often use Internet — Q39d*	(F1.0)	187-187

1 Never
2 Few times/year
3 Once/month
4 Several times/month
5 Several times/week
7 N/A
8 M/R
9 Mis

ST39Q05	*How often use science labs — Q39e*	(F1.0)	188-188

1 Never
2 Few times/year
3 Once/month
4 Several times/month
5 Several times/week
7 N/A
8 M/R
9 Mis

ST40Q01	*Job at 30 — Q40*	(A4)	189-192

9997 N/A
9999 Mis

ST41Q01	*Mark in <test lang> — Q41 numeric*	(F3.0)	193-195

997 N/A
999 Mis

ST41Q02	*Mark in <maths> — Q41 numeric*	(F3.0)	196-198

997 N/A
999 Mis

ST41Q03	*Mark in <science> — Q41 numeric*	(F3.0)	199-201

997 N/A
999 Mis

ST41Q04 *Mark in <test lang>*
- Q41 nominal (F1.0) 202-202

1 Above the pass mark
2 At the pass mark
3 Below the pass mark
7 N/A
8 M/R
9 Mis

ST41Q05 *Mark in <maths>*
- Q41nominal (F1.0) 203-203

1 Above the pass mark
2 At the pass mark
3 Below the pass mark
7 N/A
8 M/R
9 Mis

ST41Q06 *Mark in <science>*
- Q41 nominal (F1.0) 204-204

1 Above the pass mark
2 At the pass mark
3 Below the pass mark
7 N/A
8 M/R
9 Mis

ST41Q07 *Mark in <test lang>*
- Q41 ordinal (F1.0) 205-205

7 N/A
8 M/R
9 Mis

ST41Q08 *Mark in <maths>*
- Q41 ordinal (F1.0) 206-206

7 N/A
8 M/R
9 Mis

ST41Q09 *Mark in <science>*
- Q41 ordinal (F1.0) 207-207

7 N/A
8 M/R
9 Mis

BMMJ *Two-dgit SES*
Code Mother (F2.0) 209-210

97 N/A
99 Mis

BFMJ *Two-dgit SES*
Code Father (F2.0) 211-212

97 N/A
99 Mis

BTHR *Two-dgit SES Code Self* (F2.0) 213-214

97 N/A
99 Mis

IT01Q01 *At home - IT1a* (F1.0) 216-216

1 Every day
2 Few times / week
3 1-4 / month
4 < 1 / Month
5 Never
7 N/A
8 M/R
9 Mis

IT01Q02 *At school - IT1b* (F1.0) 217-217

1 Every day
2 Few times / week
3 1-4 / month
4 < 1 / Month
5 Never
7 N/A
8 M/R
9 Mis

IT01Q03 *In library - IT1c* (F1.0) 218-218

1 Every day
2 Few times / week
3 1-4 / month
4 < 1 / Month
5 Never
7 N/A
8 M/R
9 Mis

IT01Q04	*Another place - IT1d*	(F1.0)	219-219
	1	Every day	
	2	Few times / week	
	3	1-4 / month	
	4	< 1 / Month	
	5	Never	
	7	N/A	
	8	M/R	
	9	Mis	

IT02Q01	*Using - IT2a*	(F1.0)	220-220
	1	Very	
	2	Just	
	3	Somewhat	
	4	Not at all	
	7	N/A	
	8	M/R	
	9	Mis	

IT02Q02	*Write paper - IT2b*	(F1.0)	221-221
	1	Very	
	2	Just	
	3	Somewhat	
	4	Not at all	
	7	N/A	
	8	M/R	
	9	Mis	

IT02Q03	*Take test - IT2c*	(F1.0)	222-222
	1	Very	
	2	Just	
	3	Somewhat	
	4	Not at all	
	7	N/A	
	8	M/R	
	9	Mis	

IT03Q01	*Compare - IT3*	(F1.0)	223-223
	1	Excellent	
	2	Good	
	3	Fair	
	4	Poor	
	7	N/A	
	8	M/R	
	9	Mis	

IT04Q01	*At home - IT4a*	(F1.0)	224-224
	1	Every day	
	2	Few times / week	
	3	1-4 / month	
	4	< 1 / Month	
	5	Never	
	7	N/A	
	8	M/R	
	9	Mis	

IT04Q02	*At school - IT4b*	(F1.0)	225-225
	1	Every day	
	2	Few times / week	
	3	1-4 / month	
	4	< 1 / Month	
	5	Never	
	7	N/A	
	8	M/R	
	9	Mis	

IT04Q03	*In library - IT4c*	(F1.0)	226-226
	1	Every day	
	2	Few times / week	
	3	1-4 / month	
	4	< 1 / Month	
	5	Never	
	7	N/A	
	8	M/R	
	9	Mis	

IT04Q04	*Another place - IT4d*	(F1.0)	227-227
	1	Every day	
	2	Few times / week	
	3	1-4 / month	
	4	< 1 / Month	
	5	Never	
	7	N/A	
	8	M/R	
	9	Mis	

IT05Q01	*Internet - IT5a*	(F1.0) 228-228
	1 Every day	
	2 Few times / week	
	3 1-4 / month	
	4 < 1 / Month	
	5 Never	
	7 N/A	
	8 M/R	
	9 Mis	

IT05Q02	*Communication - IT5b*	(F1.0) 229-229
	1 Every day	
	2 Few times / week	
	3 1-4 / month	
	4 < 1 / Month	
	5 Never	
	7 N/A	
	8 M/R	
	9 Mis	

IT05Q03	*Help learn - IT5c*	(F1.0) 230-230
	1 Every day	
	2 Few times / week	
	3 1-4 / month	
	4 < 1 / Month	
	5 Never	
	7 N/A	
	8 M/R	
	9 Mis	

IT05Q04	*Programming - IT5d*	(F1.0) 231-231
	1 Every day	
	2 Few times / week	
	3 1-4 / month	
	4 < 1 / Month	
	5 Never	
	7 N/A	
	8 M/R	
	9 Mis	

IT06Q01	*Games - IT6a*	(F1.0) 232-232
	1 Every day	
	2 Few times / week	
	3 1-4 / month	
	4 < 1 / Month	
	5 Never	
	7 N/A	
	8 M/R	
	9 Mis	

IT06Q02	*Word proc - IT6b*	(F1.0) 233-233
	1 Every day	
	2 Few times / week	
	3 1-4 / month	
	4 < 1 / Month	
	5 Never	
	7 N/A	
	8 M/R	
	9 Mis	

IT06Q03	*Spreadsheet - IT6c*	(F1.0) 234-234
	1 Every day	
	2 Few times / week	
	3 1-4 / month	
	4 < 1 / Month	
	5 Never	
	7 N/A	
	8 M/R	
	9 Mis	

IT06Q04	*Drawing - IT6d*	(F1.0) 235-235
	1 Every day	
	2 Few times / week	
	3 1-4 / month	
	4 < 1 / Month	
	5 Never	
	7 N/A	
	8 M/R	
	9 Mis	

IT06Q05	*Educational - IT6e*	(F1.0)	236-236
1	Every day		
2	Few times / week		
3	1-4 / month		
4	< 1 / Month		
5	Never		
7	N/A		
8	M/R		
9	Mis		

IT07Q01	*Very important - IT7*	(F1.0)	237-237
1	Yes		
2	No		
7	N/A		
8	M/R		
9	Mis		

IT08Q01	*Play or work - IT8*	(F1.0)	238-238
1	Yes		
2	No		
7	N/A		
8	M/R		
9	Mis		

IT09Q01	*Very interested - IT9*	(F1.0)	239-239
1	Yes		
2	No		
7	N/A		
8	M/R		
9	Mis		

IT10Q01	*Forget the time - IT10*	(F1.0)	240-240
1	Yes		
2	No		
7	N/A		
8	M/R		
9	Mis		

CC01Q01	*Memorise - CC1/1*	(F1.0)	242-242
1	Never		
2	Some		
3	Often		
4	Always		
7	N/A		
8	M/R		
9	Mis		

CC01Q02	*Understand - CC1/2*	(F1.0)	243-243
1	Never		
2	Some		
3	Often		
4	Always		
7	N/A		
8	M/R		
9	Mis		

CC01Q03	*Need to learn - CC1/3*	(F1.0)	244-244
1	Never		
2	Some		
3	Often		
4	Always		
7	N/A		
8	M/R		
9	Mis		

CC01Q04	*Difficult - CC1/4*	(F1.0)	245-245
1	Never		
2	Some		
3	Often		
4	Always		
7	N/A		
8	M/R		
9	Mis		

CC01Q05	*Much as possible - CC1/5*	(F1.0)	246-246
1	Never		
2	Some		
3	Often		
4	Always		
7	N/A		
8	M/R		
9	Mis		

CC01Q06	*Job- CC1/6*	(F1.0)	247-247
1	Never		
2	Some		
3	Often		
4	Always		
7	N/A		
8	M/R		
9	Mis		

CC01Q07 *Work as hard - CC1/7* (F1.0) 248-248
1   Never
2   Some
3   Often
4   Always
7   N/A
8   M/R
9   Mis

CC01Q08 *Most Complex - CC1/8* (F1.0) 249-249
1   Never
2   Some
3   Often
4   Always
7   N/A
8   M/R
9   Mis

CC01Q09 *Relate New - CC1/9* (F1.0) 250-250
1   Never
2   Some
3   Often
4   Always
7   N/A
8   M/R
9   Mis

CC01Q10 *Recite - CC1/10* (F1.0) 251-251
1   Never
2   Some
3   Often
4   Always
7   N/A
8   M/R
9   Mis

CC01Q11 *Bad Grades - CC1/11* (F1.0) 252-252
1   Never
2   Some
3   Often
4   Always
7   N/A
8   M/R
9   Mis

CC01Q12 *Keep Working - CC1/12* (F1.0) 253-253
1   Never
2   Some
3   Often
4   Always
7   N/A
8   M/R
9   Mis

CC01Q13 *Force myself - CC1/13* (F1.0) 254-254
1   Never
2   Some
3   Often
4   Always
7   N/A
8   M/R
9   Mis

CC01Q14 *Future - CC1/14* (F1.0) 255-255
1   Never
2   Some
3   Often
4   Always
7   N/A
8   M/R
9   Mis

CC01Q15 *Over and over - CC1/15* (F1.0) 256-256
1   Never
2   Some
3   Often
4   Always
7   N/A
8   M/R
9   Mis

CC01Q16 *Problems wrong - CC1/16* (F1.0) 257-257
1   Never
2   Some
3   Often
4   Always
7   N/A
8   M/R
9   Mis

CC01Q17	*Real world - CC1/17*	(F1.0) 258-258
1	Never	
2	Some	
3	Often	
4	Always	
7	N/A	
8	M/R	
9	Mis	

CC01Q18	*Excellent - CC1/18*	(F1.0) 259-259
1	Never	
2	Some	
3	Often	
4	Always	
7	N/A	
8	M/R	
9	Mis	

CC01Q19	*Concepts - CC1/19*	(F1.0) 260-260
1	Never	
2	Some	
3	Often	
4	Always	
7	N/A	
8	M/R	
9	Mis	

CC01Q20	*Best to acquire - CC1/20*	(F1.0) 261-261
1	Never	
2	Some	
3	Often	
4	Always	
7	N/A	
8	M/R	
9	Mis	

CC01Q21	*Relating - CC1/21*	(F1.0) 262-262
1	Never	
2	Some	
3	Often	
4	Always	
7	N/A	
8	M/R	
9	Mis	

CC01Q22	*Good job - CC1/22*	(F1.0) 263-263
1	Never	
2	Some	
3	Often	
4	Always	
7	N/A	
8	M/R	
9	Mis	

CC01Q23	*Important- CC1/23*	(F1.0) 264-264
1	Never	
2	Some	
3	Often	
4	Always	
7	N/A	
8	M/R	
9	Mis	

CC01Q24	*Learn well - CC1/24*	(F1.0) 265-265
1	Never	
2	Some	
3	Often	
4	Always	
7	N/A	
8	M/R	
9	Mis	

CC01Q25	*Fits in - CC1/25*	(F1.0) 266-266
1	Never	
2	Some	
3	Often	
4	Always	
7	N/A	
8	M/R	
9	Mis	

CC01Q26	*Can master - CC1/26*	(F1.0) 267-267
1	Never	
2	Some	
3	Often	
4	Always	
7	N/A	
8	M/R	
9	Mis	

CC01Q27 *Additional info - CC1 / 27* (F1.0) 268-268
1   Never
2   Some
3   Often
4   Always
7   N/A
8   M/R
9   Mis

CC01Q28 *Best effort - CC1 / Q28* (F1.0) 269-269
1   Never
2   Some
3   Often
4   Always
7   N/A
8   M/R
9   Mis

CC02Q01 *Math absorbed - CC2 / 29* (F1.0) 270-270
1   Disagree
2   Disagree some
3   Agree some
4   Agree
7   N/A
8   M/R
9   Mis

CC02Q02 *Like other - CC2 / 30* (F1.0) 271-271
1   Disagree
2   Disagree some
3   Agree some
4   Agree
7   N/A
8   M/R
9   Mis

CC02Q03 *Quickly in most - CC2 / 31* (F1.0) 272-272
1   Disagree
2   Disagree some
3   Agree somc
4   Agree
7   N/A
8   M/R
9   Mis

CC02Q04 *Better - CC2 / 32* (F1.0) 273-273
1   Disagree
2   Disagree some
3   Agree some
4   Agree
7   N/A
8   M/R
9   Mis

CC02Q05 *Hopeless - CC2 / 33* (F1.0) 274-274
1   Disagree
2   Disagree some
3   Agree some
4   Agree
7   N/A
8   M/R
9   Mis

CC02Q06 *Reading fun - CC2 / 34* (F1.0) 275-275
1   Disagree
2   Disagree some
3   Agree some
4   Agree
7   N/A
8   M/R
9   Mis

CC02Q07 *Good most - CC2 / 35* (F1.0) 276-276
1   Disagree
2   Disagree some
3   Agree some
4   Agree
7   N/A
8   M/R
9   Mis

CC02Q08 *Learn most - CC2 / 36* (F1.0) 277-277
1   Disagree
2   Disagree some
3   Agree some
4   Agree
7   N/A
8   M/R
9   Mis

CC02Q09 *Learn quickly - CC2/37* (F1.0)   278-278
1   Disagree
2   Disagree some
3   Agree some
4   Agree
7   N/A
8   M/R
9   Mis

CC02Q10 *Math fun - CC2/38*   (F1.0) 279-279
1   Disagree
2   Disagree some
3   Agree some
4   Agree
7   N/A
8   M/R
9   Mis

CC02Q11 *Trying better - CC2/39* (F1.0) 280-280
1   Disagree
2   Disagree some
3   Agree some
4   Agree
7   N/A
8   M/R
9   Mis

CC02Q12 *Good marks Math*
- CC2/Q40   (F1.0)   281-281
1   Disagree
2   Disagree some
3   Agree some
4   Agree
7   N/A
8   M/R
9   Mis

CC02Q13 *Read spare - CC2/41*   (F1.0) 282-282
1   Disagree
2   Disagree some
3   Agree some
4   Agree
7   N/A
8   M/R
9   Mis

CC02Q14 *Best work - CC2/42*   (F1.0)   283-283
1   Disagree
2   Disagree some
3   Agree some
4   Agree
7   N/A
8   M/R
9   Mis

CC02Q15 *Math best - CC2/43*   (F1.0)   284-284
1   Disagree
2   Disagree some
3   Agree some
4   Agree
7   N/A
8   M/R
9   Mis

CC02Q16 *Like to be best - CC2/44*(F1.0)   285-285
1   Disagree
2   Disagree some
3   Agree some
4   Agree
7   N/A
8   M/R
9   Mis

CC02Q17 *Read absorbed - CC2/45* (F1.0) 286-286
1   Disagree
2   Disagree some
3   Agree some
4   Agree
7   N/A
8   M/R
9   Mis

CC02Q18 *Done well - CC2/46*   (F1.0) 287-287
1   Disagree
2   Disagree some
3   Agree some
4   Agree
7   N/A
8   M/R
9   Mis

CC02Q19   *Help others - CC2/47*   (F1.0)   288-288
1   Disagree
2   Disagree some
3   Agree some
4   Agree
7   N/A
8   M/R
9   Mis

CC02Q20   *Well in tests - CC2/48*   (F1.0)   289-289
1   Disagree
2   Disagree some
3   Agree some
4   Agree
7   N/A
8   M/R
9   Mis

CC02Q21   *Math important - CC2/49*   (F1.0)   290-290
1   Disagree
2   Disagree some
3   Agree some
4   Agree
7   N/A
8   M/R
9   Mis

CC02Q22   *Helpful ideas - CC2/50*   (F1.0)   291-291
1   Disagree
2   Disagree some
3   Agree some
4   Agree
7   N/A
8   M/R
9   Mis

CC02Q23   *Good marks - CC2/51*   (F1.0)   292-292
1   Disagree
2   Disagree some
3   Agree some
4   Agree
7   N/A
8   M/R
9   Mis

CC02Q24   *Learn faster - CC2/52*   (F1.0)   293-293
1   Disagree
2   Disagree some
3   Agree some
4   Agree
7   N/A
8   M/R
9   Mis

RMINS   *Minutes per week in language courses*   (F4.0)   295-298
9997 N/A
9999 Mis

MMINS   *Minutes per week in math courses*   (F4.0)   299-302
9997 N/A
9999 Mis

SMINS   *Minutes per week in science courses*   (F4.0)   303-306
9997 N/A
9999 Mis

AGE   *Student age in months*   (F3.0)   307-309
997   Mis
997   N/A
998   Invalid A

FAMSTRUC   *Family structure*   (F1.0)   310-310
1   Single
2   Nuclear
3   Mixed
4   Other
7   Not Applicable
9   Missing

NSIB   *Number of siblings*   (F2.0)   311-312
97   N/A
98   Mis
99   Mis

BRTHORD   *Birth oer*   (F1.0)   313-313
7   N/A
8   Mis
9   Mis

ISEI	Int. Socio-Econ Index of father or mother	(F2.0)	314-315
	97 N/A		
	98 Mis		
	99 Mis		
HISEI	Highest Int. Socio-Econ. Index	(F2.0)	316-317
	97 N/A		
	98 Mis		
	99 Mis		
FISCED	Father ISCED qualification	(F1.0)	318-318
	7 N/A		
	8 Mis		
	9 Mis		
MISCED	Mother ISCED qualification	(F1.0)	319-319
	7 N/A		
	8 Mis		
	9 Mis		
CULTCOM	Cultural communication	(F5.2)	321-325
	97 N/A		
SOCCOM	Social communication	(F5.2)	326-330
	97 N/A		
FAMEDSUP	Family educational support	(F5.2)	331-335
	97 N/A		
WEALTH	Family wealth	(F5.2)	336-340
	97 N/A		
HEDRES	Home educational resources	(F5.2)	341-345
	97 N/A		
CULTACTV	Cultural activities of students	(F5.2)	346-350
	97 N/A		
CULTPOSS	Cultural possession of the family	(F5.2)	351-355
	97 N/A		
HMWKTIME	Time spent on homework	(F5.2)	356-360
	97 N/A		

TEACHSUP	Teacher support	(F5.2)	361-365
	97 N/A		
DISCLIMA	School disciplinary climate	(F5.2)	366-370
	97 N/A		
STUDREL	Teacher-student relationship	(F5.2)	371-375
	97 N/A		
ACHPRESS	Achievement press	(F5.2)	376-380
	97 N/A		
BELONG	Sense of belonging	(F5.2)	381-385
	97 N/A		
JOYREAD	Enjoyment of Reading	(F5.2)	386-390
	97 N/A		
DIVREAD	Reading diversity	(F5.2)	391-395
	97 N/A		
COMAB	Confort and ability with computer	(F5.2)	397-401
	97 N/A		
COMUSE	Computer usage and experience	(F5.2)	402-406
	97 N/A		
COMATT	Attitudes toward computers	(F5.2)	407-411
	97 N/A		
CSTRAT	Control strategies	(F5.2)	412-416
	97 N/A		
EFFPER	Effort and perseverance	(F5.2)	417-421
	97 N/A		
MEMOR	Memorisation	(F5.2)	422-426
	97 N/A		
SELFEF	Self efficacy	(F5.2)	427-431
	97 N/A		
CEXP	Control expectation	(F5.2)	432-437
	97 N/A		
ELAB	Elaboration	(F5.2)	437-441
	97 N/A		
INSMOT	Instrumental motivation	(F5.2)	442-446
	97 N/A		

INTMAT	*Interest in Maths* 97 N/A	(F5.2)	447-451
MATCON	*Mathematics self concept* 97 N/A	(F5.2)	452-456
INTREA	*Interest in reading* 97 N/A	(F5.2)	457-461
SCACAD	*Self concept (academic)* 97 N/A	(F5.2)	462-466
SCVERB	*Self concept (verbal)* 97 N/A	(F5.2)	467-471
COMLRN	*Competitive learning* 97 N/A	(F5.2)	472-476
COPLRN	*Co-operative learning* 97 N/A	(F5.2)	477-481
WLEMATH	*Warm estimate in mathematics* 9997 N/A	(F7.2)	483-489
WLERR_M	*WLE measurement error for mathematics* 9997 N/A	(F7.2)	490-496
WLEREAD	*Warm estimate in reading* 9997 N/A	(F7.2)	497-503
WLERR_R	*WLE measurement error for reading* 9997 N/A	(F7.2)	504-510
WLEREAD1	*Warm estimate in reading - retrieving* 9997 N/A	(F7.2)	511-517
WLERR_R1	*WLE measurement error for reading 1* 9997 N/A	(F7.2)	518-524
WLEREAD2	*Warm estimate in reading - interpreting* 9997 N/A	(F7.2)	525-531
WLERR_R2	*WLE measurement error for reading 2* 9997 N/A	(F7.2)	532-538

WLEREAD3	*Warm estimate in reading - reflecting* 9997 N/A	(F7.2)	539-545
WLERR_R3	*WLE measurement error for reading 3* 9997 N/A	(F7.2)	546-552
WLESCIE	*Warm estimate in science* 9997 N/A	(F7.2)	553-559
WLERR_S	*WLE measurement error for science* 9997 N/A	(F7.2)	560-566
PV1MATH	*Plausible value in mathematics* 9997 N/A	(F7.2)	568-574
PV2MATH	*Plausible value in mathematics* 9997 N/A	(F7.2)	575-581
PV3MATH	*Plausible value in mathematics* 9997 N/A	(F7.2)	582-588
PV4MATH	*Plausible value in mathematics* 9997 N/A	(F7.2)	589-595
PV5MATH	*Plausible value in mathematics* 9997 N/A	(F7.2)	596-602
PV1READ	*Plausible value in reading* 9997 N/A	(F7.2)	603-609
PV2READ	*Plausible value in reading* 9997 N/A	(F7.2)	610-616
PV3READ	*Plausible value in reading* 9997 N/A	(F7.2)	617-623
PV4READ	*Plausible value in reading* 9997 N/A	(F7.2)	624-630
PV5READ	*Plausible value in reading* 9997 N/A	(F7.2)	631-637

PV1READ1	*Plausible value in reading - retrieving* 9997 N/A	(F7.2)	638-644
PV2READ1	*Plausible value in reading - retrieving* 9997 N/A	(F7.2)	645-651
PV3READ1	*Plausible value in reading - retrieving* 9997 N/A	(F7.2)	652-658
PV4READ1	*Plausible value in reading - retrieving* 9997 N/A	(F7.2)	659-665
PV5READ1	*Plausible value in reading - retrieving* 9997 N/A	(F7.2)	666-672
PV1READ2	*Plausible value in reading- interpreting* 9997 N/A	(F7.2)	673-679
PV2READ2	*Plausible value in reading- interpreting* 9997 N/A	(F7.2)	680-686
PV3READ2	*Plausible value in reading- interpreting* 9997 N/A	(F7.2)	687-693
PV4READ2	*Plausible value in reading- interpreting* 9997 N/A	(F7.2)	694-700
PV5READ2	*Plausible value in reading- interpreting* 9997 N/A	(F7.2)	701-707
PV1READ3	*Plausible value in reading - reflecting* 9997 N/A	(F7.2)	708-714
PV2READ3	*Plausible value in reading - reflecting* 9997 N/A	(F7.2)	715-721
PV3READ3	*Plausible value in reading - reflecting* 9997 N/A	(F7.2)	722-728

PV4READ3	*Plausible value in reading - reflecting* 9997 N/A	(F7.2)	729-735
PV5READ3	*Plausible value in reading - reflecting* 9997 N/A	(F7.2)	736-742
PV1SCIE	*Plausible value in science* 9997 N/A	(F7.2)	743-749
PV2SCIE	*Plausible value in science* 9997 N/A	(F7.2)	750-756
PV3SCIE	*Plausible value in science* 9997 N/A	(F7.2)	757-763
PV4SCIE	*Plausible value in science* 9997 N/A	(F7.2)	764-770
PV5SCIE	*Plausible value in science* 9997 N/A	(F7.2)	771-777
W_FSTUWT	*Student final weight*	(F9.4)	779-789
W_MFAC	*Weight adjustment factor for Mathematics*	(F9.4)	788-796
W_SFAC	*Weight adjustment factor for Science*	(F9.4)	797-805
CNTMFAC	*Country Math adjustment factor*	(F9.7)	806-814
CNTRFAC	*Country Reading adjustment factor*	(F9.7)	815-823
CNTSFAC	*Country Science adjustment factor*	(F9.7)	824-832
W_FSTR1	*BRR replicate*	(F9.4)	834-842
W_FSTR2	*BRR replicate*	(F9.4)	843-851
W_FSTR3	*BRR replicate*	(F9.4)	852-860
W_FSTR4	*BRR replicate*	(F9.4)	861-869
W_FSTR5	*BRR replicate*	(F9.4)	870-878
W_FSTR6	*BRR replicate*	(F9.4)	879-887
W_FSTR7	*BRR replicate*	(F9.4)	888-896
W_FSTR8	*BRR replicate*	(F9.4)	897-905

W_FSTR9	BRR replicate	(F9.4)	906-914	W_FSTR40	BRR replicate	(F9.4)	1185-1193
W_FSTR10	BRR replicate	(F9.4)	915-923	W_FSTR41	BRR replicate	(F9.4)	1194-1202
W_FSTR11	BRR replicate	(F9.4)	924-932	W_FSTR42	BRR replicate	(F9.4)	1203-1211
W_FSTR12	BRR replicate	(F9.4)	933-941	W_FSTR43	BRR replicate	(F9.4)	1212-1220
W_FSTR13	BRR replicate	(F9.4)	942-950	W_FSTR44	BRR replicate	(F9.4)	1221-1229
W_FSTR14	BRR replicate	(F9.4)	951-959	W_FSTR45	BRR replicate	(F9.4)	1230-1238
W_FSTR15	BRR replicate	(F9.4)	960-968	W_FSTR46	BRR replicate	(F9.4)	1239-1247
W_FSTR16	BRR replicate	(F9.4)	969-977	W_FSTR47	BRR replicate	(F9.4)	1248-1256
W_FSTR17	BRR replicate	(F9.4)	978-986	W_FSTR48	BRR replicate	(F9.4)	1257-1265
W_FSTR18	BRR replicate	(F9.4)	987-995	W_FSTR49	BRR replicate	(F9.4)	1266-1274
W_FSTR19	BRR replicate	(F9.4)	996-1004	W_FSTR50	BRR replicate	(F9.4)	1275-1283
W_FSTR20	BRR replicate	(F9.4)	1005-1013	W_FSTR51	BRR replicate	(F9.4)	1284-1292
W_FSTR21	BRR replicate	(F9.4)	1014-1022	W_FSTR52	BRR replicate	(F9.4)	1293-1301
W_FSTR22	BRR replicate	(F9.4)	1023-1031	W_FSTR53	BRR replicate	(F9.4)	1302-1310
W_FSTR23	BRR replicate	(F9.4)	1032-1040	W_FSTR54	BRR replicate	(F9.4)	1311-1319
W_FSTR24	BRR replicate	(F9.4)	1041-1049	W_FSTR55	BRR replicate	(F9.4)	1320-1328
W_FSTR25	BRR replicate	(F9.4)	1050-1058	W_FSTR56	BRR replicate	(F9.4)	1329-1337
W_FSTR26	BRR replicate	(F9.4)	1059-1067	W_FSTR57	BRR replicate	(F9.4)	1338-1346
W_FSTR27	BRR replicate	(F9.4)	1068-1076	W_FSTR58	BRR replicate	(F9.4)	1347-1355
W_FSTR28	BRR replicate	(F9.4)	1077-1085	W_FSTR59	BRR replicate	(F9.4)	1356-1364
W_FSTR29	BRR replicate	(F9.4)	1086-1094	W_FSTR60	BRR replicate	(F9.4)	1365-1373
W_FSTR30	BRR replicate	(F9.4)	1095-1103	W_FSTR61	BRR replicate	(F9.4)	1374-1382
W_FSTR31	BRR replicate	(F9.4)	1104-1112	W_FSTR62	BRR replicate	(F9.4)	1383-1391
W_FSTR32	BRR replicate	(F9.4)	1113-1121	W_FSTR63	BRR replicate	(F9.4)	1392-1400
W_FSTR33	BRR replicate	(F9.4)	1122-1130	W_FSTR64	BRR replicate	(F9.4)	1401-1409
W_FSTR34	BRR replicate	(F9.4)	1131-1139	W_FSTR65	BRR replicate	(F9.4)	1410-1418
W_FSTR35	BRR replicate	(F9.4)	1140-1148	W_FSTR66	BRR replicate	(F9.4)	1419-1427
W_FSTR36	BRR replicate	(F9.4)	1149-1157	W_FSTR67	BRR replicate	(F9.4)	1428-1436
W_FSTR37	BRR replicate	(F9.4)	1158-1166	W_FSTR68	BRR replicate	(F9.4)	1437-1445
W_FSTR38	BRR replicate	(F9.4)	1167-1175	W_FSTR69	BRR replicate	(F9.4)	1446-1454
W_FSTR39	BRR replicate	(F9.4)	1176-1184	W_FSTR70	BRR replicate	(F9.4)	1455-1463

W_FSTR71	*BRR replicate*	(F9.4)	1464-1472
W_FSTR72	*BRR replicate*	(F9.4)	1473-1481
W_FSTR73	*BRR replicate*	(F9.4)	1482-1490
W_FSTR74	*BRR replicate*	(F9.4)	1491-1499
W_FSTR75	*BRR replicate*	(F9.4)	1500-1508
W_FSTR76	*BRR replicate*	(F9.4)	1509-1517
W_FSTR77	*BRR replicate*	(F9.4)	1518-1526
W_FSTR78	*BRR replicate*	(F9.4)	1527-1535
W_FSTR79	*BRR replicate*	(F9.4)	1536-1544
W_FSTR80	*BRR replicate*	(F9.4)	1545-1553
CNT	*Country alphanumerical code*	(A3)	1555-1557

APPENDIX 6 **SCHOOL QUESTIONNAIRE CODEBOOK**

COUNTRY	Country three-digit code	(A3)	2-4
SCHOOLID	School ID (unique)	(A5)	5-9
SUBNATIO	Subnational entities	(A2)	11-12

SC01Q01 *School location - Q1* (F1.0) 14-14
1 Village (less 3 000)
2 Small town (3 000 to 15 000)
3 Town (15 000 to 100 000)
4 City (100 000 to 1 000 000)
5 City (more 1 000 000) centre
6 City (more 1 000 000) elswhere
7 N/A
8 M/R
9 Mis

SC02Q01 *Number of boys - Q2a* (F4.0) 15-18
9997 N/A
9999 Mis

SC02Q02 *Number of girls - Q2b* (F4.0) 19-22
9997 N/A
9999 Mis

SC03Q01 *School public/private - Q3* (F1.0) 23-23
1 Public
2 Private
7 N/A
8 M/R
9 Mis

SC04Q01 *Funds, government - Q4a* (F3.0) 24-26
997 N/A
999 Mis

SC04Q02 *Funds, student fees - Q4b* (F3.0) 27-29
997 N/A
999 Mis

SC04Q03 *Funds, benefactors - Q4c* (F3.0) 30-32
997 N/A
999 Mis

SC04Q04 *Funds, other - Q4d* (F3.0) 33-35
997 N/A
999 Mis

SC05Q01 *Grade 1 - Q5a* (F1.0) 36-36
1 Yes
2 No
7 N/A
8 M/R
9 Mis

SC05Q02 *Grade 2 - Q5b* (F1.0) 37-37
1 Yes
2 No
7 N/A
8 M/R
9 Mis

SC05Q03 *Grade 3 - Q5c* (F1.0) 38-38
1 Yes
2 No
7 N/A
8 M/R
9 Mis

SC05Q04 *Grade 4 - Q5d* (F1.0) 39-39
1 Yes
2 No
7 N/A
8 M/R
9 Mis

SC05Q05 *Grade 5 - Q5e* (F1.0) 40-40
1 Yes
2 No
7 N/A
8 M/R
9 Mis

SC05Q06 *Grade 6 - Q5f* (F1.0) 41-41
1 Yes
2 No
7 N/A
8 M/R
9 Mis

SC05Q07 *Grade 7 - Q5g* (F1.0) 42-42
1   Yes
2   No
7   N/A
8   M/R
9   Mis

SC05Q08 *Grade 8 - Q5h* (F1.0) 43-43
1   Yes
2   No
7   N/A
8   M/R
9   Mis

SC05Q09 *Grade 9 - Q5i* (F1.0) 44-44
1   Yes
2   No
7   N/A
8   M/R
9   Mis

SC05Q10 *Grade 10 - Q5j* (F1.0) 45-45
1   Yes
2   No
7   N/A
8   M/R
9   Mis

SC05Q11 *Grade 11 - Q5k* (F1.0) 46-46
1   Yes
2   No
7   N/A
8   M/R
9   Mis

SC05Q12 *Grade 12 - Q5l* (F1.0) 47-47
1   Yes
2   No
7   N/A
8   M/R
9   Mis

SC05Q13 *Grade 13 - Q5m* (F1.0) 48-48
1   Yes
2   No
7   N/A
8   M/R
9   Mis

SC05Q14 *Ungraded- Q5n* (F1.0) 49-49
1   Yes
2   No
7   N/A
8   M/R
9   Mis

SC06Q01 *Instructional weeks - Q6a* (F2.0) 50-51
97   N/A
99   Mis

SC06Q02 *Instructional periods - Q6b* (F2.0) 52-53
97   N/A
99   Mis

SC06Q03 *Instructional minutes - Q6c* (F3.0) 54-56
997   N/A
999   Mis

SC07Q01 *Residence - Q7a* (F1.0) 57-57
1   Never
2   Sometimes
3   Always
7   N/A
8   M/R
9   Mis

SC07Q02 *Academic performance - Q7b* (F1.0) 58-58
1   Never
2   Sometimes
3   Always
7   N/A
8   M/R
9   Mis

SC07Q03 *Feeder schools - Q7c* (F1.0) 59-59
1   Never
2   Sometimes
3   Always
7   N/A
8   M/R
9   Mis

SC07Q04 *Phylosophy and religion - Q7d* (F1.0) 60-60
1   Never
2   Sometimes
3   Always
7   N/A
8   M/R
9   Mis

SC07Q05 *Special program - Q7e*   (F1.0) 61-61
1   Never
2   Sometimes
3   Always
7   N/A
8   M/R
9   Mis

SC07Q06 *Family preference - Q7f*   (F1.0) 62-62
1   Never
2   Sometimes
3   Always
7   N/A
8   M/R
9   Mis

SC07Q07 *Admittance factors, other - Q7g* (F1.0) 63-63
1   Never
2   Sometimes
3   Always
7   N/A
8   M/R
9   Mis

SC08Q01 *<ISCED 2A> - Q8a*   (F3.0) 64-66
997   N/A
999   Mis

SC08Q02 *<ISCED 2B> - Q8b*   (F3.0) 67-69
997   N/A
999   Mis

SC08Q03 *<ISCED 2C> - Q8c*   (F3.0) 70-72
997   N/A
999   Mis

SC08Q04 *<ISCED 3A> - Q8d*   (F3.0) 73-75
997   N/A
999   Mis

SC08Q05 *<ISCED 3B> - Q8e*   (F3.0) 76-78
997   N/A
999   Mis

SC08Q06 *<ISCED 3C> - Q8f*   (F3.0) 79-81
997   N/A
999   Mis

SC09Q01 *Student's choice - Q9a*   (F1.0) 82-82
1   Not important
2   Important
3   Very important
7   N/A
8   M/R
9   Mis

SC09Q02 *Academic record - Q9b*   (F1.0) 83-83
1   Not important
2   Important
3   Very important
7   N/A
8   M/R
9   Mis

SC09Q03 *Placement exams - Q9c*   (F1.0) 84-84
1   Not important
2   Important
3   Very important
7   N/A
8   M/R
9   Mis

SC09Q04 *Teacher recommend - Q9d* (F1.0) 85-85
1   Not important
2   Important
3   Very important
7   N/A
8   M/R
9   Mis

SC09Q05 *Parents' request - Q9e*   (F1.0) 86-86
1   Not important
2   Important
3   Very important
7   N/A
8   M/R
9   Mis

SC10Q01 *Low achievement - Q10a*   (F1.0) 87-87
1   Not likely
2   Likely
3   Very likely
7   N/A
8   M/R
9   Mis

SC10Q02 *High achievement - Q10b* (F1.0) 88-88
1   Not likely
2   Likely
3   Very likely
7   N/A
8   M/R
9   Mis

SC10Q03 *Behaviour - Q10c*   (F1.0) 89-89
1   Not likely
2   Likely
3   Very likely
7   N/A
8   M/R
9   Mis

SC10Q04 *Special needs - Q10d*   (F1.0) 90-90
1   Not likely
2   Likely
3   Very likely
7   N/A
8   M/R
9   Mis

SC10Q05 *Parents' request -Q10e*   (F1.0) 91-91
1   Not likely
2   Likely
3   Very likely
7   N/A
8   M/R
9   Mis

SC10Q06 *Transfer reason, other - Q10f* (F1.0) 92-92
1   Not likely
2   Likely
3   Very likely
7   N/A
8   M/R
9   Mis

SC11Q01 *Poor buildings - Q11a*   (F1.0) 93-93
1   Not at all
2   A little
3   Some
4   A lot
7   N/A
8   M/R
9   Mis

SC11Q02 *Poor heating - Q11b*   (F1.0) 94-94
1   Not at all
2   A little
3   Some
4   A lot
7   N/A
8   M/R
9   Mis

SC11Q03 *Inadequate space - Q11c* (F1.0) 95-95
1   Not at all
2   A little
3   Some
4   A lot
7   N/A
8   M/R
9   Mis

SC11Q04 *Lack of instruct
materials - Q11d*   (F1.0) 96-96
1   Not at all
2   A little
3   Some
4   A lot
7   N/A
8   M/R
9   Mis

SC11Q05 *Lack of computers - Q11e* (F1.0) 97-97
1   Not at all
2   A little
3   Some
4   A lot
7   N/A
8   M/R
9   Mis

SC11Q06	Poor library - Q11f	(F1.0)	98-98
	1	Not at all	
	2	A little	
	3	Some	
	4	A lot	
	7	N/A	
	8	M/R	
	9	Mis	
SC11Q07	Poor multi-media Q11g	(F1.0)	99-99
	1	Not at all	
	2	A little	
	3	Some	
	4	A lot	
	7	N/A	
	8	M/R	
	9	Mis	
SC11Q08	Poor science equip - Q11h	(F1.0)	100-100
	1	Not at all	
	2	A little	
	3	Some	
	4	A lot	
	7	N/A	
	8	M/R	
	9	Mis	
SC11Q09	Poor art facilities - Q11i	(F1.0)	101-101
	1	Not at all	
	2	A little	
	3	Some	
	4	A lot	
	7	N/A	
	8	M/R	
	9	Mis	
SC12Q01	Courses for gifted - Q12a	(F1.0)	102-102
	1	Yes	
	2	No	
	7	N/A	
	8	M/R	
	9	Mis	

SC12Q02	Language training - Q12b	(F1.0)	103-103
	1	Yes	
	2	No	
	7	N/A	
	8	M/R	
	9	Mis	
SC12Q03	Study skills - Q12c	(F1.0)	104-104
	1	Yes	
	2	No	
	7	N/A	
	8	M/R	
	9	Mis	
SC12Q04	Special tutoring - Q12d	(F1.0)	105-105
	1	Yes	
	2	No	
	7	N/A	
	8	M/R	
	9	Mis	
SC12Q05	Help rooms - Q12e	(F1.0)	106-106
	1	Yes	
	2	No	
	7	N/A	
	8	M/R	
	9	Mis	
SC13Q01	Computers altogether - Q13a	(F4.0)	107-110
	9997	N/A	
	9999	Mis	
SC13Q02	Computers students - Q13b	(F4.0)	111-114
	9997	N/A	
	9999	Mis	
SC13Q03	Computers teachers - Q13c	(F4.0)	115-118
	9997	N/A	
	9999	Mis	
SC13Q04	Computers admin - Q13d	(F4.0)	119-122
	9997	N/A	
	9999	Mis	
SC13Q05	Computers withWeb - Q13e	(F4.0)	123-126
	9997	N/A	
	9999	Mis	

SC13Q06 *Computers with Lan - Q13f* (F4.0) 127-130
9997 N/A
9999 Mis

SC14Q01 *Ftime teach in total - Q14a1* (F3.0) 131-133
997 N/A
999 Mis

SC14Q02 *Ptime teach in total - Q14a2* (F3.0) 134-136
997 N/A
999 Mis

SC14Q03 *Ftime teach <ISCED5A>*
in <pedag> - Q14b1 (F3.0) 137-139
997 N/A
999 Mis

SC14Q04 *Ptime teach <ISCED5A>*
in <pedag> - Q14b2 (F3.0) 140-142
997 N/A
999 Mis

SC14Q05 *Ftime teach*
fully certified - Q14c1 (F3.0) 143-145
997 N/A
999 Mis

SC14Q06 *Ptime teach*
fully certified - Q14c2 (F3.0) 146-148
997 N/A
999 Mis

SC14Q07 *Ftime teach*
<test language> - Q14d1 (F3.0) 149-151
997 N/A
999 Mis

SC14Q08 *Ptime teach*
<test language> - Q14d2 (F3.0) 152-154
997 N/A
999 Mis

SC14Q09 *Ftime teach <ISCED5A>*
in <test lang> - Q14e1 (F3.0) 155-157
997 N/A
999 Mis

SC14Q10 *Ptime teach <ISCED5A>*
in <test lang> - Q14e2 (F3.0) 158-160
997 N/A
999 Mis

SC14Q11 *Ftime teach*
<maths> - Q14f1 (F3.0) 161-163
997 N/A
999 Mis

SC14Q12 *Ptime teach*
<maths> - Q14f2 (F3.0) 164-166
997 N/A
999 Mis

SC14Q13 *Ftime teach <ISCED5A>*
in <maths> - Q14g1 (F3.0) 167-169
997 N/A
999 Mis

SC14Q14 *Ptime teach <ISCED5A>*
in <maths> - Q14g2 (F3.0) 170-172
997 N/A
999 Mis

SC14Q15 *Ftime teach*
<science> - Q14h1 (F3.0) 173-175
997 N/A
999 Mis

SC14Q16 *Ptime teach*
<science> - Q14h2 (F3.0) 176-178
997 N/A
999 Mis

SC14Q17 *Ftime teach <ISCED5A>*
in <science> - Q14i1 (F3.0) 179-181
997 N/A
999 Mis

SC14Q18 *Ptime teach - <ISCED5A>*
in <science> - Q14i2 (F3.0) 182-184
997 N/A
999 Mis

SC15Q01 *Professional*
development - Q15 (F3.0) 185-187
997 N/A
999 Mis

SC16Q01 *Standardised test - Q16a* (F1.0) 188-188

1 Never
2 Yearly
3 Twice a year
4 3 times a year
5 4 or more times a year
7 N/A
8 M/R
9 Mis

SC16Q02 *Teacher's test - Q16b* (F1.0) 189-189

1 Never
2 Yearly
3 Twice a year
4 3 times a year
5 4 or more times a year
7 N/A
8 M/R
9 Mis

SC16Q03 *Teacher's ratings - Q16c* (F1.0) 190-190

1 Never
2 Yearly
3 Twice a year
4 3 times a year
5 4 or more times a year
7 N/A
8 M/R
9 Mis

SC16Q04 *Students' portfolios - Q16d* (F1.0) 191-191

1 Never
2 Yearly
3 Twice a year
4 3 times a year
5 4 or more times a year
7 N/A
8 M/R
9 Mis

SC16Q05 *Assignments - Q16e* (F1.0) 192-192

1 Never
2 Yearly
3 Twice a year
4 3 times a year
5 4 or more times a year
7 N/A
8 M/R
9 Mis

SC17Q01 *Parents - Q17a* (F1.0) 193-193

1 Never
2 Yearly
3 Twice a year
4 3 times a year
5 4 or more times a year
7 N/A
8 M/R
9 Mis

SC17Q02 *Principal - Q17b* (F1.0) 194-194

1 Never
2 Yearly
3 Twice a year
4 3 times a year
5 4 or more times a year
7 N/A
8 M/R
9 Mis

SC17Q03 *Government - Q17c* (F1.0) 195-195

1 Never
2 Yearly
3 Twice a year
4 3 times a year
5 4 or more times a year
7 N/A
8 M/R
9 Mis

SC18Q01	*Parents information - Q18a* (F1.0) 196-196	
	1	Yes
	2	No
	7	N/A
	8	M/R
	9	Mis

SC18Q02	*Promotion decisions - Q18b* (F1.0) 197-197	
	1	Yes
	2	No
	7	N/A
	8	M/R
	9	Mis

SC18Q03	*Instructional grouping - Q18c* (F1.0) 198-198	
	1	Yes
	2	No
	7	N/A
	8	M/R
	9	Mis

SC18Q04	*National comparison - Q18d* (F1.0) 199-199	
	1	Yes
	2	No
	7	N/A
	8	M/R
	9	Mis

SC18Q05	*Progress monitoring - Q18e* (F1.0) 200-200	
	1	Yes
	2	No
	7	N/A
	8	M/R
	9	Mis

SC18Q06	*Teachers' effectiveness -Q18f* (F1.0) 201-201	
	1	Yes
	2	No
	7	N/A
	8	M/R
	9	Mis

SC19Q01	*Low expectations - Q19a* (F1.0) 202-202	
	1	Not at all
	2	A little
	3	Some
	4	A lot
	7	N/A
	8	M/R
	9	Mis

SC19Q02	*Student absenteeism - Q19b* (F1.0) 203-203	
	1	Not at all
	2	A little
	3	Some
	4	A lot
	7	N/A
	8	M/R
	9	Mis

SC19Q03	*Stud-teach relations - Q19c* (F1.0) 204-204	
	1	Not at all
	2	A little
	3	Some
	4	A lot
	7	N/A
	8	M/R
	9	Mis

SC19Q04	*Teacher turnover - Q19d* (F1.0) 205-205	
	1	Not at all
	2	A little
	3	Some
	4	A lot
	7	N/A
	8	M/R
	9	Mis

SC19Q05	*Lack parent support - Q19e* (F1.0) 206-206	
	1	Not at all
	2	A little
	3	Some
	4	A lot
	7	N/A
	8	M/R
	9	Mis

SC19Q06	*Disruptions of classes - Q19f*	(F1.0) 207-207
	1	Not at all
	2	A little
	3	Some
	4	A lot
	7	N/A
	8	M/R
	9	Mis

SC19Q07	*Ignoring students - Q19g*	(F1.0) 208-208
	1	Not at all
	2	A little
	3	Some
	4	A lot
	7	N/A
	8	M/R
	9	Mis

SC19Q08	*Teacher absenteeism - Q19h*	(F1.0) 209-209
	1	Not at all
	2	A little
	3	Some
	4	A lot
	7	N/A
	8	M/R
	9	Mis

SC19Q09	*Skipping classes - Q19i*	(F1.0) 210-210
	1	Not at all
	2	A little
	3	Some
	4	A lot
	7	N/A
	8	M/R
	9	Mis

SC19Q10	*Lack of respect -Q19j*	(F1.0) 211-211
	1	Not at all
	2	A little
	3	Some
	4	A lot
	7	N/A
	8	M/R
	9	Mis

SC19Q11	*Resisting change - Q19k*	(F1.0) 212-212
	1	Not at all
	2	A little
	3	Some
	4	A lot
	7	N/A
	8	M/R
	9	Mis

SC19Q12	*Lack of instr time - Q19l*	(F1.0) 213-213
	1	Not at all
	2	A little
	3	Some
	4	A lot
	7	N/A
	8	M/R
	9	Mis

SC19Q13	*Use of alcohol - Q19m*	(F1.0) 214-214
	1	Not at all
	2	A little
	3	Some
	4	A lot
	7	N/A
	8	M/R
	9	Mis

SC19Q14	*Teachers' strictness - Q19n*	(F1.0) 215-215
	1	Not at all
	2	A little
	3	Some
	4	A lot
	7	N/A
	8	M/R
	9	Mis

SC19Q15	*Bullying - Q19o*	(F1.0) 216-216
	1	Not at all
	2	A little
	3	Some
	4	A lot
	7	N/A
	8	M/R
	9	Mis

SC19Q16   *Lack of encouragm - Q19p*   (F1.0)   217-217
1   Not at all
2   A little
3   Some
4   A lot
7   N/A
8   M/R
9   Mis

SC19Q17   *Poor home envrm - Q19q*   (F1.0)   218-218
1   Not at all
2   A little
3   Some
4   A lot
7   N/A
8   M/R
9   Mis

SC20Q01   *High morale -Q20a*   (F1.0)   219-219
1   Strongly Disagree
2   Disagree
3   Agree
4   Strongly Agree
7   N/A
8   M/R
9   Mis

SC20Q02   *Enthusiasm -Q20b*   (F1.0)   220-220
1   Strongly Disagree
2   Disagree
3   Agree
4   Strongly Agree
7   N/A
8   M/R
9   Mis

SC20Q03   *Pride in school -Q20c*   (F1.0)   221-221
1   Strongly Disagree
2   Disagree
3   Agree
4   Strongly Agree
7   N/A
8   M/R
9   Mis

SC20Q04   *Value acad achvm -Q20d*   (F1.0)   222-222
1   Strongly Disagree
2   Disagree
3   Agree
4   Strongly Agree
7   N/A
8   M/R
9   Mis

SC21Q01   *Teachers - Q21a*   (F1.0)   223-223
1   Not at all
2   A little
3   Some
4   A lot
7   N/A
8   M/R
9   Mis

SC21Q02   *<Test language>*
teachers - Q21b   (F1.0)   224-224
1   Not at all
2   A little
3   Some
4   A lot
7   N/A
8   M/R
9   Mis

SC21Q03   *<Mathematics>*
teacher - Q21c   (F1.0)   225-225
1   Not at all
2   A little
3   Some
4   A lot
7   N/A
8   M/R
9   Mis

SC21Q04   *<Science> teachers - Q21d* (F1.0)   226-226
1   Not at all
2   A little
3   Some
4   A lot
7   N/A
8   M/R
9   Mis

SC21Q05	Support personnel - Q21e	(F1.0)	227-227
1	Not at all		
2	A little		
3	Some		
4	A lot		
7	N/A		
8	M/R		
9	Mis		

SC22Q01	Hiring teachers - Q22a	(A5)	228-232
99997 N/A			
99999 Mis			

SC22Q02	Firing teachers - Q22b	(A5)	233-237
99997 N/A			
99999 Mis			

SC22Q03	Teacher salaries - Q22c	(A5)	238-242
99997 N/A			
99999 Mis			

SC22Q04	Salary increase -Q22d	(A5)	243-247
99997 N/A			
99999 Mis			

SC22Q05	Budget formulation - Q22e	(A5)	248-252
99997 N/A			
99999 Mis			

SC22Q06	Budget allocation - Q22f	(A5)	253-257
99997 N/A			
99999 Mis			

SC22Q07	Disciplinary policies - Q22g	(A5)	258-262
99997 N/A			
99999 Mis			

SC22Q08	Assessment policies - Q22h	(A5)	263-267
99997 N/A			
99999 Mis			

SC22Q09	Student admittance - Q22i	(A5)	268-272
99997 N/A			
99999 Mis			

SC22Q10	Textbooks - Q22j	(A5)	273-277
99997 N/A			
99999 Mis			

SC22Q11	Course content - Q22k	(A5)	278-282
99997 N/A			
99999 Mis			

SC22Q12	Course offer - Q22l	(A5)	283-287
99997 N/A			
99999 Mis			

SCHLSIZE	Number of students in the school	(F5.0)	289-293
99997 N/A			
99999 Mis			

PCGIRLS	Percentage of girls in the school	(F5.3)	294-298
7	N/A		
9	Mis		

SCHLTYPE	Type of school	(F1.0)	299-299
1	Private, government independent		
2	Private, government dependent		
3	Government		
7	N/A		
9	Mis		

TOTHRS	Total number of schooling hours per	(F4.0)	300-303
9997	N/A		
9999	Mis		

RATCOMP	Total number of computer / school size	(F6.3)	304-309
997	N/A		
999	Mis		

PERCOMP1	% of computers available to 15-year-olds	(F4.2)	310-313
7	N/A		
7	N/A		

PERCOMP2	% of computers available only for teachers	(F4.2)	314-317
7	N/A		
9	Mis		

PERCOMP3	% of computers available for administrative staff	(F4.2)	318-321
7	N/A		
9	Mis		

PERCOMP4 *% of computers connected*
to the Web (F4.2) 322-325
7 N/A
9 Mis

PERCOMP5 *% of computers connected*
to a LAN (F4.2) 326-329
7 N/A
9 Mis

STRATIO *School size / number*
of teachers (F5.2) 330-334
97 N/A
99 Mis

PROPQUAL *Prop of teachers with*
ISCED5A level in pedagogy (F4.2) 335-338
7 N/A
9 Mis

PROPCERT *Prop of teachers*
fully certified (F4.2) 339-342
7 N/A
9 Mis

PROPREAD *Prop of language teachers with ISCED5A level*
in pedagogy (F4.2) 343-346
7 N/A
9 Mis

PROPMATH *Prop of math teachers with ISCED5A level*
in mathematics (F4.2) 347-350
7 N/A
9 Mis

PROPSCIE *Prop of science teachers with ISCED5A level*
in science (F4.2) 351-354
7 N/A
9 Mis

SCMATEDU *Instructional resources* (F5.2) 355-359
97 N/A

TCSHORT *Shortage of teachers* (F5.2) 360-364
97 N/A

TEACBEHA *Teacher behaviors* (F5.2) 365-369
97 N/A

STUDBEHA *Student behaviors* (F5.2) 370-374
97 N/A

TCMORALE *Teacher morale* (F5.2) 375-379
97 N/A

SCHAUTON *School autonomy* (F5.2) 380-384
97 N/A

TCHPARTI *Teacher participation to*
decision making (F5.2) 385-389
97 N/A

SCMATBUI *Material ressources* (F5.2) 390-394
97 N/A

WNRSCHBW *School weight* (F8.2) 395-402

CNT *Country alphanumeric code* (A3) 404-406

APPENDIX 7 *STUDENT TEST DATA CODEBOOK*

COUNTR	*Country ID*		(A4)	1-4
SCHOOLID	*School ID (unique)*		(A5)	5-9
STIDSTD	*Student ID*		(A5)	10-14
SUBNATIO	*Subnational entities*		(A2)	16-17
BOOKID	*Booklet Number*		(A2)	19-20

M033Q01	*ViewRoom – Q1*		MC	(A1)	22-22
	1 No credit	*Booklet 0*		*Q11*	
	2 No credit	*Booklet 3*		*Q47*	
	3 No credit	*Booklet 5*		*Q58*	
	4 Full Credit	*Booklet 9*		*Q26*	
	8 M/R				
	9 Missing				
	n N/A				
	r Not reached				

M034Q01T	*Bricks – Q1*		FR	(A1)	23-23
	0 No credit	*Booklet 3*		*Q48*	
	1 Full Credit	*Booklet 5*		*Q59*	
	9 Missing	*Booklet 9*		*Q27*	
	n N/A				
	r Not reached				

M037Q01T	*Farms – Q1*		FR	(A1)	24-24
	0 No credit	*Booklet 1*		*Q52*	
	1 Full Credit	*Booklet 9*		*Q22*	
	9 Missing				
	n N/A				
	r Not reached				

M037Q02T	*Farms – Q2*		FR	(A1)	25-25
	0 No credit	*Booklet 1*		*Q53*	
	1 Full Credit	*Booklet 9*		*Q23*	
	9 Missing				
	n N/A				
	r Not reached				

M124Q01	*Walking – Q1*		FR	(A1)	26-26
	0 No credit	*Booklet 1*		*Q54*	
	1 No credit	*Booklet 9*		*Q24*	
	2 Full Credit				
	9 Missing				
	n N/A				
	r Not reached				

M124Q03T	*Walking – Q3*		FR	(A1)	27-27
	0 No credit	*Booklet 1*		*Q55*	
	1 Partial Credit	*Booklet 9*		*Q25*	
	2 Partial Credit				
	3 Full Credit				
	9 Missing				
	n N/A				
	r Not reached				
M136Q01T	*Apples – Q1*		FR	(A1)	28-28
	0 No credit	*Booklet 1*		*Q56*	
	1 No credit	*Booklet 5*		*Q50*	
	2 Full Credit	*Booklet 8*		*Q9*	
	9 Missing				
	n N/A				
	r Not reached				
M136Q02T	*Apples – Q2*		FR	(A1)	29-29
	0 No credit	*Booklet 1*		*Q57*	
	1 Full Credit	*Booklet 5*		*Q51*	
	9 Missing	*Booklet 8*		*Q10*	
	n N/A				
	r Not reached				
M136Q03T	*Apples – Q3*		FR	(A1)	30-30
	0 No credit	*Booklet 1*		*Q58*	
	1 Partial Credit	*Booklet 5*		*Q52*	
	2 Full Credit	*Booklet 8*		*Q11*	
	9 Missing				
	n N/A				
	r Not reached				
M144Q01T	*Cube Painting – Q1*		FR	(A1)	31-31
	0 No credit	*Booklet 0*		*Q13*	
	1 Full Credit	*Booklet 1*		*Q48*	
	9 Missing	*Booklet 9*		*Q18*	
	n N/A				
	r Not reached				
M144Q02T	*Cube Painting – Q2*		FR	(A1)	32-32
	0 No credit	*Booklet 1*		*Q49*	
	1 Full Credit	*Booklet 9*		*Q19*	
	9 Missing				
	n N/A				
	r Not reached				

M144Q03	Cube Painting – Q3		MC	(A1)	33-33
	1 Full Credit	Booklet 0		Q14	
	2 No credit	Booklet 1		Q50	
	3 No credit	Booklet 9		Q20	
	4 No credit				
	8 M/R				
	9 Missing				
	n N/A				
	r Not reached				
M144Q04T	Cube Painting – Q4		FR	(A1)	34-34
	0 No credit	Booklet 1		Q51	
	1 Full Credit	Booklet 9		Q21	
	9 Missing				
	n N/A				
	r Not reached				
M145Q01T	Cubes – Q1		FR	(A1)	35-35
	0 No credit	Booklet 0		Q12	
	1 Full Credit	Booklet 3		Q54	
	9 Missing	Booklet 5		Q65	
	n N/A	Booklet 9		Q33	
	r Not reached				
M148Q02T	Continent Area		FR	(A1)	36-36
	0 No credit	Booklet 1		Q60	
	1 Partial Credit	Booklet 5		Q54	
	2 Full Credit	Booklet 8		Q13	
	9 Missing				
	n N/A				
	r Not reached				
M150Q01T	Growing Up – Q1		FR	(A1)	37-37
	0 No credit	Booklet 0		Q18	
	1 Full Credit	Booklet 1		Q61	
	9 Missing	Booklet 5		Q55	
	n N/A	Booklet 8		Q14	
	r Not reached				
M150Q02T	Growing Up – Q2		FR	(A1)	38-38
	0 No credit	Booklet 0		Q20	
	1 Partial Credit	Booklet 1		Q63	
	2 Full Credit	Booklet 5		Q57	
	9 Missing	Booklet 8		Q16	
	n N/A				
	r Not reached				

M150Q03T	*Growing Up – Q3*		FR	(A1)	39-39
	0 No credit	*Booklet 0*		*Q19*	
	1 Full Credit	*Booklet 1*		*Q62*	
	9 Missing	*Booklet 5*		*Q56*	
	n N/A	*Booklet 8*		*Q15*	
	r Not reached				

M155Q01	*Pop Pyramids – Q1*		FR	(A1)	40-40
	0 No credit	*Booklet 3*		*Q50*	
	1 Full Credit	*Booklet 5*		*Q61*	
	9 Missing	*Booklet 9*		*Q29*	
	n N/A				
	r Not reached				

M155Q02T	*Pop Pyramids – Q2*		FR	(A1)	41-41
	0 No credit	*Booklet 3*		*Q49*	
	1 Partial Credit	*Booklet 5*		*Q60*	
	2 Full Credit	*Booklet 9*		*Q28*	
	9 Missing				
	n N/A				
	r Not reached				

M155Q03T	*Pop Pyramids – Q3*		FR	(A1)	42-42
	0 No credit	*Booklet 3*		*Q51*	
	1 Partial Credit	*Booklet 5*		*Q62*	
	2 Full Credit	*Booklet 9*		*Q30*	
	9 Missing				
	n N/A				
	r Not reached				

M155Q04T	*Pop Pyramids – Q4*		CMC	(A1)	43-43
	0 No credit	*Booklet 3*		*Q52*	
	1 No credit	*Booklet 5*		*Q63*	
	2 No credit	*Booklet 9*		*Q31*	
	3 No credit				
	4 Full Credit				
	8 M/R				
	9 Missing				
	n N/A				
	r Not reached				

M159Q01	*Racing Car – Q1*		MC	(A1) 44-44
	1 No credit	*Booklet 0*		*Q15*
	2 Full Credit	*Booklet 3*		*Q55*
	3 No credit	*Booklet 8*		*Q1*
	4 No credit			
	8 M/R			
	9 Missing			
	n N/A			
	r Not reached			
M159Q02	*Racing Car – Q2*		MC	(A1) 45-45
	1 No credit	*Booklet 0*		*Q16*
	2 No credit	*Booklet 3*		*Q56*
	3 Full Credit	*Booklet 8*		*Q2*
	4 No credit			
	8 M/R			
	9 Missing			
	n N/A			
	r Not reached			
M159Q03	*Racing Car – Q3*		MC	(A1) 46-46
	1 No credit	*Booklet 0*		*Q17*
	2 Full Credit	*Booklet 3*		*Q57*
	3 No credit	*Booklet 8*		*Q3*
	4 No credit			
	8 M/R			
	9 Missing			
	n N/A			
	r Not reached			
M159Q05	*Racing Car – Q5*		MC	(A1) 47-47
	1 No credit	*Booklet 3*		*Q58*
	2 Full Credit	*Booklet 8*		*Q4*
	3 No credit			
	4 No credit			
	5 No credit			
	8 M/R			
	9 Missing			
	n N/A			
	r Not reached			

M161Q01	*Triangles — Q1*		MC	(A1)	48-48
	1 No credit	*Booklet 3*		*Q62*	
	2 No credit	*Booklet 8*		*Q8*	
	3 No credit				
	4 Full Credit				
	5 No credit				
	8 M/R				
	9 Missing				
	n N/A				
	r Not reached				
M179Q01T	*Robberies — Q1*		FR	(A1)	49-49
	0 No credit	*Booklet 3*		*Q61*	
	1 Partial Credit	*Booklet 8*		*Q7*	
	2 Full Credit				
	9 Missing				
	n N/A				
	r Not reached				
M192Q01T	*Containers — Q1*		CMC	(A1)	50-50
	0 No credit	*Booklet 3*		*Q53*	
	1 No credit	*Booklet 5*		*Q64*	
	2 Full Credit	*Booklet 9*		*Q32*	
	3 Full Credit				
	8 M/R				
	9 Missing				
	n N/A				
	r Not reached				
M266Q01T	*Carpenter — Q01*		CMC	(A1)	51-51
	0 No credit	*Booklet 3*		*Q59*	
	1 No credit	*Booklet 8*		*Q5*	
	2 No credit				
	3 No Credit				
	4 Full Credit				
	8 M/R				
	9 Missing				
	n N/A				
	r Not reached				
M273Q01T	*Pipelines — Q1*		CMC	(A1)	52-52
	0 No credit	*Booklet 3*		*Q60*	
	1 Full Credit	*Booklet 8*		*Q6*	
	9 Missing				
	n N/A				
	r Not reached				

R040Q02	*Lake Chad – Q2*		MC	(A1)	53-53
	1 Full Credit	*Booklet 8*		Q62	
	2 No Credit	*Booklet 9*		Q49	
	3 No Credit				
	4 No Credit				
	5 No Credit				
	8 M/R				
	9 Missing				
	n N/A				
	r Not reached				
R040Q03A	*Lake Chad – Q3A*		FR	(A1)	54-54
	0 No credit	*Booklet 8*		Q63	
	1 Full Credit	*Booklet 9*		Q50	
	9 Missing				
	n N/A				
	r Not reached				
R040Q03B	*Lake Chad – Q3B*		FR	(A1)	55-55
	0 No credit	*Booklet 8*		Q64	
	1 Full Credit	*Booklet 9*		Q51	
	9 Missing				
	n N/A				
	r Not reached				
R040Q04	*Lake Chad – Q4*		MC	(A1)	56-56
	1 Full Credit	*Booklet 8*		Q65	
	2 No Credit	*Booklet 9*		Q52	
	3 No Credit				
	4 No Credit				
	8 M/R				
	9 Missing				
	n N/A				
	r Not reached				
R040Q06	*Lake Chad – Q6*		MC	(A1)	57-57
	1 No Credit	*Booklet 8*		Q66	
	2 No Credit	*Booklet 9*		Q53	
	3 Full Credit				
	4 No Credit				
	8 M/R				
	9 Missing				
	n N/A				
	r Not reached				

R055Q01	*DruggedSpiders*		MC	(A1)	58-58
	1 No Credit	*Booklet 2*		*Q26*	
	2 No Credit	*Booklet 4*		*Q21*	
	3 No Credit	*Booklet 5*		*Q3*	
	4 Full Credit				
	8 M/R				
	9 Missing				
	n N/A				
	r Not reached				
R055Q02	*DruggedSpiders*		FR	(A1)	59-59
	0 No credit	*Booklet 2*		*Q27*	
	1 Full Credit	*Booklet 4*		*Q22*	
	9 Missing	*Booklet 5*		*Q4*	
	n N/A				
	r Not reached				
R055Q03	*DruggedSpiders*		FR	(A1)	60-60
	0 No credit	*Booklet 2*		*Q28*	
	1 No credit	*Booklet 4*		*Q23*	
	2 Full Credit	*Booklet 5*		*Q5*	
	9 Missing				
	n N/A				
	r Not reached				
R055Q05	*DruggedSpiders*		FR	(A1)	61-61
	0 No credit	*Booklet 2*		*Q29*	
	1 Full Credit	*Booklet 4*		*Q24*	
	9 Missing	*Booklet 5*		*Q6*	
	n N/A				
	r Not reached				
R061Q01	*Macondo – Q1*		FR	(A1)	62-62
	0 No credit	*Booklet 3*		*Q30*	
	1 Full Credit	*Booklet 5*		*Q16*	
	2 Full Credit				
	9 Missing				
	n N/A				
	r Not reached				
R061Q03	*Macondo – Q3*		MC	(A1)	63-63
	1 No Credit	*Booklet 3*		*Q31*	
	2 No Credit	*Booklet 5*		*Q17*	
	3 Full Credit	*Booklet 6*		*Q2*	
	4 No Credit				
	8 M/R				
	9 Missing				
	n N/A				
	r Not reached				

R061Q04	*Macondo — Q4*		MC	(A1)	64-64
	1 No Credit	*Booklet 3*		Q32	
	2 No Credit	*Booklet 5*		Q18	
	3 Full Credit	*Booklet 6*		Q3	
	4 No Credit				
	8 M/R				
	9 Missing				
	n N/A				
	r Not reached				
R061Q05	*Macondo — Q5*		FR	(A1)	65-65
	0 No credit	*Booklet 3*		Q33	
	1 Full Credit	*Booklet 5*		Q19	
	9 Missing	*Booklet 6*		Q4	
	n N/A				
	r Not reached				
R067Q01	*Aesop — Q1*		MC	(A1)	66-66
	1 No Credit	*Booklet 2*		Q33	
	2 No Credit	*Booklet 4*		Q28	
	3 Full Credit	*Booklet 5*		Q10	
	4 No Credit				
	8 M/R				
	9 Missing				
	n N/A				
	r Not reached				
R067Q04	*Aesop — Q4*		FR	(A1)	67-67
	0 No credit	*Booklet 2*		Q34	
	1 Partial Credit	*Booklet 4*		Q29	
	2 Full Credit	*Booklet 5*		Q11	
	9 Missing				
	n N/A				
	r Not reached				
R067Q05	*Aesop — Q5*		FR	(A1)	68-68
	0 No credit	*Booklet 2*		Q35	
	1 Partial Credit	*Booklet 4*		Q30	
	2 Full Credit	*Booklet 5*		Q12	
	9 Missing				
	n N/A				
	r Not reached				

R070Q02	*Beach — Q2*		MC	(A1)	69-69
	1 Full Credit	*Booklet 1*		*Q17*	
	2 No Credit	*Booklet 5*		*Q49*	
	3 No Credit	*Booklet 7*		*Q33*	
	4 No Credit				
	8 M/R				
	9 Missing				
	n N/A				
	r Not reached				
R070Q03	*Beach — Q3*		MC	(A1)	70-70
	1 No Credit	*Booklet 1*		*Q15*	
	2 No Credit	*Booklet 5*		*Q47*	
	3 Full Credit	*Booklet 7*		*Q31*	
	4 No Credit				
	8 M/R				
	9 Missing				
	n N/A				
	r Not reached				
R070Q04	*Beach — Q4*		FR	(A1)	71-71
	0 No credit	*Booklet 1*		*Q16*	
	1 Full Credit	*Booklet 5*		*Q48*	
	9 Missing	*Booklet 7*		*Q32*	
	n N/A				
	r Not reached				
R070Q07T	*Beach — Q7*		CMC	(A1)	72-72
	0 No credit	*Booklet 1*		*Q14*	
	1 No credit	*Booklet 5*		*Q46*	
	2 No credit	*Booklet 7*		*Q30*	
	3 No credit				
	4 Partial Credit				
	5 Full Credit				
	8 M/R				
	9 Missing				
	n N/A				
	r Not reached				
R076Q03	*Iran Air — Q3*		FR	(A1)	73-73
	0 No credit	*Booklet 2*		*Q36*	
	1 Full Credit	*Booklet 4*		*Q31*	
	9 Missing	*Booklet 5*		*Q13*	
	n N/A				
	r Not reached				

R076Q04	*Iran Air — Q4*		FR	(A1)	74-74
	0 No credit	*Booklet 2*		Q37	
	1 Full Credit	*Booklet 4*		Q32	
	9 Missing	*Booklet 5*		Q14	
	n N/A				
	r Not reached				
R076Q05	*Iran Air — Q5*		MC	(A1)	75-75
	1 Full Credit	*Booklet 2*		Q38	
	2 No Credit	*Booklet 4*		Q33	
	3 No Credit	*Booklet 5*		Q15	
	4 No Credit				
	5 No Credit				
	8 M/R				
	9 Missing				
	n N/A				
	r Not reached				
R077Q02	*Flu — Q2*		MC	(A1)	76-76
	1 No Credit	*Booklet 8*		Q47	
	2 Full Credit	*Booklet 9*		Q34	
	3 No Credit				
	4 No Credit				
	8 M/R				
	9 Missing				
	n N/A				
	r Not reached				
R077Q03	*Flu — Q3*		FR	(A1)	77-77
	0 No credit	*Booklet 8*		Q48	
	1 Partial Credit	*Booklet 9*		Q35	
	2 Full Credit				
	9 Missing				
	n N/A				
	r Not reached				
R077Q04	*Flu — Q4*		MC	(A1)	78-78
	1 No Credit	*Booklet 8*		Q49	
	2 Full Credit	*Booklet 9*		Q36	
	3 No Credit				
	4 No Credit				
	8 M/R				
	9 Missing				
	n N/A				
	r Not reached				

R077Q05	*Flu – Q5*		FR	(A1)	79-79
	0 No credit	*Booklet 8*		Q50	
	1 No credit	*Booklet 9*		Q37	
	2 Full Credit				
	9 Missing				
	n N/A				
	r Not reached				
R077Q06	*Flu – Q6*		MC	(A1)	80-80
	1 No Credit	*Booklet 8*		Q51	
	2 No Credit	*Booklet 9*		Q38	
	3 No Credit				
	4 Full Credit				
	8 M/R				
	9 Missing				
	n N/A				
	r Not reached				
R081Q01	*Graffiti – Q1*		MC	(A1)	81-81
	1 No Credit	*Booklet 1*		Q3	
	2 Full Credit	*Booklet 5*		Q35	
	3 No Credit	*Booklet 7*		Q19	
	4 No Credit				
	8 M/R				
	9 Missing				
	n N/A				
	r Not reached				
R081Q05	*Graffiti – Q5*		FR	(A1)	82-82
	0 No credit	*Booklet 1*		Q5	
	1 Full Credit	*Booklet 5*		Q37	
	9 Missing	*Booklet 7*		Q21	
	n N/A				
	r Not reached				
R081Q06A	*Graffiti – Q6A*		FR	(A1)	83-83
	0 No credit	*Booklet 1*		Q6	
	1 Full Credit	*Booklet 5*		Q38	
	9 Missing	*Booklet 7*		Q22	
	n N/A				
	r Not reached				
R081Q06B	*Graffiti – Q6B*		FR	(A1)	84-84
	0 No credit	*Booklet 1*		Q7	
	1 Full Credit	*Booklet 5*		Q39	
	9 Missing	*Booklet 7*		Q23	
	n N/A				
	r Not reached				

R083Q01	*Household – Q1*		MC	(A1)	85-85
	1 No Credit	*Booklet 3*		*Q34*	
	2 No Credit	*Booklet 5*		*Q20*	
	3 No Credit	*Booklet 6*		*Q5*	
	4 Full Credit				
	8 M/R				
	9 Missing				
	n N/A				
	r Not reached				

R083Q02	*Household – Q2*		FR	(A1)	86-86
	0 No credit	*Booklet 3*		*Q35*	
	1 Full Credit	*Booklet 5*		*Q21*	
	9 Missing	*Booklet 6*		*Q6*	
	n N/A				
	r Not reached				

R083Q03	*Household – Q3*		FR	(A1)	87-87
	0 No credit	*Booklet 3*		*Q36*	
	1 Full Credit	*Booklet 5*		*Q22*	
	9 Missing	*Booklet 6*		*Q7*	
	n N/A				
	r Not reached				

R083Q04	*Household – Q4*		MC	(A1)	88-88
	1 Full Credit	*Booklet 3*		*Q37*	
	2 No Credit	*Booklet 5*		*Q23*	
	3 No Credit	*Booklet 6*		*Q8*	
	4 No Credit				
	8 M/R				
	9 Missing				
	n N/A				
	r Not reached				

R083Q06	*Household – Q6*		FR	(A1)	89-89
	0 No credit	*Booklet 3*		*Q38*	
	1 Full Credit	*Booklet 5*		*Q24*	
	9 Missing	*Booklet 6*		*Q9*	
	n N/A				
	r Not reached				

R086Q04	*If – Q4*		FR	(A1)	90-90
	0 No credit	*Booklet 1*		*Q37*	
	1 Full Credit	*Booklet 3*		*Q19*	
	9 Missing	*Booklet 4*		*Q8*	
	n N/A				
	r Not reached				

R086Q05	*If – Q5*		MC	(A1)	91-91
	1 No Credit	*Booklet 1*		Q35	
	2 No Credit	*Booklet 3*		Q17	
	3 Full Credit	*Booklet 4*		Q6	
	4 No Credit				
	8 M/R				
	9 Missing				
	n N/A				
	r Not reached				
R086Q07	*If – Q7*		FR	(A1)	92-92
	0 No credit	*Booklet 1*		Q36	
	1 Full Credit	*Booklet 3*		Q18	
	9 Missing	*Booklet 4*		Q7	
	n N/A				
	r Not reached				
R088Q01	*Labour – Q1*		MC	(A1)	93-93
	1 No Credit	*Booklet 8*		Q57	
	2 No Credit	*Booklet 9*		Q44	
	3 No Credit				
	4 Full Credit				
	8 M/R				
	9 Missing				
	n N/A				
	r Not reached				
R088Q03	*Labour – Q3*		FR	(A1)	94-94
	0 No credit	*Booklet 8*		Q58	
	1 Partial Credit	*Booklet 8*		Q58	
	2 Full Credit	*Booklet 9*		Q45	
	9 Missing	*Booklet 9*		Q45	
	n N/A				
	r Not reached				
R088Q04T	*Labour – Q4*		CMC	(A1)	95-95
	0 No credit	*Booklet 8*		Q59	
	1 No credit	*Booklet 9*		Q46	
	2 No credit				
	3 Partial Credit				
	4 Partial Credit				
	5 Full Credit				
	8 M/R				
	9 Missing				
	n N/A				
	r Not reached				

R088Q05T	*Labour — Q5*		CMC	(A1)	96-96
	0 No credit	*Booklet 8*		*Q60*	
	1 No credit	*Booklet 9*		*Q47*	
	2 No credit				
	3 Full Credit				
	8 M/R				
	9 Missing				
	n N/A				
	r Not reached				
R088Q07	*Labour — Q7*		MC	(A1)	97-97
	1 No Credit	*Booklet 8*		*Q61*	
	2 No Credit	*Booklet 9*		*Q48*	
	3 Full Credit				
	4 No Credit				
	8 M/R				
	9 Missing				
	n N/A				
	r Not reached				
R091Q05	*Library — Q5*		FR	(A1)	98-98
	0 No credit	*Booklet 2*		*Q13*	
	1 Full Credit	*Booklet 3*		*Q1*	
	9 Missing	*Booklet 7*		*Q34*	
	n N/A				
	r Not reached				
R091Q06	*Library — Q6*		MC	(A1)	99-99
	1 No Credit	*Booklet 2*		*Q14*	
	2 Full Credit	*Booklet 3*		*Q2*	
	3 No Credit	*Booklet 7*		*Q35*	
	4 No Credit				
	8 M/R				
	9 Missing				
	n N/A				
	r Not reached				
R091Q07B	*Library — Q7B*		FR	(A1)	100-100
	0 No credit	*Booklet 2*		*Q16*	
	1 No credit	*Booklet 3*		*Q4*	
	2 Full Credit	*Booklet 7*		*Q37*	
	9 Missing				
	n N/A				
	r Not reached				

R093Q03	*News Agencies -Q3*		FR	(A1)	101-101
	0 No credit	*Booklet 2*		Q24	
	1 Full Credit	*Booklet 4*		Q19	
	9 Missing	*Booklet 5*		Q1	
	n N/A				
	r Not reached				
R099Q04B	*Planint – Q4B*		FR	(A1)	102-102
	0 No credit	*Booklet 4*		Q39	
	1 No credit	*Booklet 6*		Q23	
	2 Partial Credit	*Booklet 7*		Q6	
	3 Full Credit				
	9 Missing				
	n N/A				
	r Not reached				
R100Q04	*Police – Q4*		MC	(A1)	103-103
	1 No Credit	*Booklet 3*		Q39	
	2 Full Credit	*Booklet 5*		Q25	
	3 No Credit	*Booklet 6*		Q10	
	4 No Credit				
	8 M/R				
	9 Missing				
	n N/A				
	r Not reached				
R100Q05	*Police – Q5*		MC	(A1)	104-104
	1 No Credit	*Booklet 3*		Q40	
	2 No Credit	*Booklet 5*		Q26	
	3 Full Credit	*Booklet 6*		Q11	
	4 No Credit				
	8 M/R				
	9 Missing				
	n N/A				
	r Not reached				
R100Q06	*Police – Q6*		MC	(A1)	105-105
	1 No Credit	*Booklet 3*		Q41	
	2 No Credit	*Booklet 5*		Q27	
	3 Full Credit	*Booklet 6*		Q12	
	4 No Credit				
	8 M/R				
	9 Missing				
	n N/A				
	r Not reached				

R100Q07	*Police — Q7*		MC	(A1)	106-106
	1 No Credit	*Booklet 3*		*Q42*	
	2 Full Credit	*Booklet 5*		*Q28*	
	3 No Credit	*Booklet 6*		*Q13*	
	4 No Credit				
	8 M/R				
	9 Missing				
	n N/A				
	r Not reached				
R101Q01	*Rhinoceros — Q1*		MC	(A1)	107-107
	1 No Credit	*Booklet 1*		*Q8*	
	2 No Credit	*Booklet 5*		*Q40*	
	3 Full Credit	*Booklet 7*		*Q24*	
	4 No Credit				
	8 M/R				
	9 Missing				
	n N/A				
	r Not reached				
R101Q02	*Rhinoceros — Q2*		MC	(A1)	108-108
	1 No Credit	*Booklet 1*		*Q9*	
	2 Full Credit	*Booklet 5*		*Q41*	
	3 No Credit	*Booklet 7*		*Q25*	
	4 No Credit				
	8 M/R				
	9 Missing				
	n N/A				
	r Not reached				
R101Q03	*Rhinoceros — Q3*		MC	(A1)	109-109
	1 No Credit	*Booklet 1*		*Q10*	
	2 Full Credit	*Booklet 5*		*Q42*	
	3 No Credit	*Booklet 7*		*Q26*	
	4 No Credit				
	8 M/R				
	9 Missing				
	n N/A				
	r Not reached				
R101Q04	*Rhinoceros — Q4*		MC	(A1)	110-110
	1 No Credit	*Booklet 1*		*Q11*	
	2 No Credit	*Booklet 5*		*Q43*	
	3 Full Credit	*Booklet 7*		*Q27*	
	4 No Credit				
	8 M/R				
	9 Missing				
	n N/A				
	r Not reached				

R101Q05	*Rhinoceros – Q5*		MC	(A1)	111-111
	1 No Credit	*Booklet 1*		*Q12*	
	2 No Credit	*Booklet 5*		*Q44*	
	3 No Credit	*Booklet 7*		*Q28*	
	4 Full Credit				
	8 M/R				
	9 Missing				
	n N/A				
	r Not reached				
R101Q08	*Rhinoceros – Q8*		MC	(A1)	112-112
	1 No Credit	*Booklet 1*		*Q13*	
	2 No Credit	*Booklet 5*		*Q45*	
	3 Full Credit	*Booklet 7*		*Q29*	
	4 No Credit				
	8 M/R				
	9 Missing				
	n N/A				
	r Not reached				
R102Q01	*Shirt – Q1*		MC	(A1)	113-113
	1 No Credit	*Booklet 1*		*Q38*	
	2 Full Credit	*Booklet 3*		*Q20*	
	3 No Credit	*Booklet 4*		*Q9*	
	4 No Credit				
	8 M/R				
	9 Missing				
	n N/A				
	r Not reached				
R102Q04A	*Shirt – Q4A*		FR	(A1)	114-114
	0 No credit	*Booklet 1*		*Q39*	
	1 Full Credit	*Booklet 3*		*Q21*	
	9 Missing	*Booklet 4*		*Q10*	
	n N/A				
	r Not reached				
R102Q05	*Shirt – Q5*		FR	(A1)	115-115
	0 No credit	*Booklet 1*		*Q40*	
	1 Full Credit	*Booklet 3*		*Q22*	
	9 Missing	*Booklet 4*		*Q11*	
	n N/A				
	r Not reached				

R102Q06	*Shirt – Q6*		FR	(A1)	116-116
	0 No credit	*Booklet 1*		*Q41*	
	1 Full Credit	*Booklet 3*		*Q23*	
	9 Missing	*Booklet 4*		*Q12*	
	n N/A				
	r Not reached				
R102Q07	*Shirt – Q7*		MC	(A1)	117-117
	1 No Credit	*Booklet 1*		*Q42*	
	2 No Credit	*Booklet 3*		*Q24*	
	3 Full Credit	*Booklet 4*		*Q13*	
	4 No Credit				
	8 M/R				
	9 Missing				
	n N/A				
	r Not reached				
R104Q01	*Telephone – Q1*		FR	(A1)	118-118
	0 No credit	*Booklet 3*		*Q43*	
	1 Full Credit	*Booklet 5*		*Q29*	
	9 Missing	*Booklet 6*		*Q14*	
	n N/A				
	r Not reached				
R104Q02	*Telephone – Q2*		FR	(A1)	119-119
	0 No credit	*Booklet 3*		*Q44*	
	1 Full Credit	*Booklet 5*		*Q30*	
	9 Missing	*Booklet 6*		*Q15*	
	n N/A				
	r Not reached				
R104Q05	*Telephone – Q5*		FR	(A1)	120-120
	0 No credit	*Booklet 3*		*Q46*	
	1 Partial Credit	*Booklet 5*		*Q32*	
	2 Full Credit	*Booklet 6*		*Q17*	
	9 Missing				
	n N/A				
	r Not reached				
R104Q06	*Telephone – Q6*		FR	(A1)	121-121
	0 No credit	*Booklet 3*		*Q45*	
	1 Full Credit	*Booklet 5*		*Q31*	
	9 Missing	*Booklet 6*		*Q16*	
	n N/A				
	r Not reached				

R110Q01	*Runners — Q1*		MC	(A1)	122-122
	1 No Credit	*Booklet 0*		*Q7*	
	2 No Credit	*Booklet 7*		*Q45*	
	3 No Credit	*Booklet 8*		*Q35*	
	4 Full Credit	*Booklet 9*		*Q54*	
	8 M/R				
	9 Missing				
	n N/A				
	r Not reached				
R110Q04	*Runners — Q4*		FR	(A1)	123-123
	0 No credit	*Booklet 0*		*Q8*	
	1 Full Credit	*Booklet 7*		*Q46*	
	9 Missing	*Booklet 8*		*Q36*	
	n N/A	*Booklet 9*		*Q55*	
	r Not reached				
R110Q05	*Runners — Q5*		FR	(A1)	124-124
	0 No credit	*Booklet 0*		*Q9*	
	1 Full Credit	*Booklet 7*		*Q47*	
	9 Missing	*Booklet 8*		*Q37*	
	n N/A	*Booklet 9*		*Q56*	
	r Not reached				
R110Q06	*Runners — Q6*		MC	(A1)	125-125
	1 No Credit	*Booklet 0*		*Q10*	
	2 No Credit	*Booklet 7*		*Q48*	
	3 No Credit	*Booklet 8*		*Q38*	
	4 Full Credit	*Booklet 9*		*Q57*	
	8 M/R				
	9 Missing				
	n N/A				
	r Not reached				
R111Q01	*Exchange — Q1*		MC	(A1)	126-126
	1 No Credit	*Booklet 1*		*Q43*	
	2 No Credit	*Booklet 3*		*Q25*	
	3 No Credit	*Booklet 4*		*Q14*	
	4 Full Credit				
	8 M/R				
	9 Missing				
	n N/A				
	r Not reached				

R111Q02B	*Exchange – Q2B*		FR	(A1)	127-127
	0 No credit	*Booklet 1*		Q44	
	1 Partial Credit	*Booklet 3*		Q26	
	2 Full Credit	*Booklet 4*		Q15	
	9 Missing				
	n N/A				
	r Not reached				

R111Q04	*Exchange – Q4*		MC	(A1)	128-128
	1 No Credit	*Booklet 1*		Q45	
	2 No Credit	*Booklet 3*		Q27	
	3 Full Credit	*Booklet 4*		Q16	
	4 No Credit				
	8 M/R				
	9 Missing				
	n N/A				
	r Not reached				

R111Q06B	*Exchange – Q6B*		FR	(A1)	129-129
	0 No credit	*Booklet 1*		Q47	
	1 Partial Credit	*Booklet 3*		Q29	
	2 Full Credit	*Booklet 4*		Q18	
	9 Missing				
	n N/A				
	r Not reached				

R119Q01	*Gift – Q1*		MC	(A1)	130-130
	1 No Credit	*Booklet 2*		Q18	
	2 No Credit	*Booklet 3*		Q6	
	3 Full Credit	*Booklet 7*		Q39	
	4 No Credit				
	8 M/R				
	9 Missing				
	n N/A				
	r Not reached				

R119Q04	*Gift – Q4*		MC	(A1)	131-131
	1 No Credit	*Booklet 2*		Q22	
	2 No Credit	*Booklet 3*		Q10	
	3 Full Credit	*Booklet 7*		Q43	
	4 No Credit				
	8 M/R				
	9 Missing				
	n N/A				
	r Not reached				

R119Q05	*Gift – Q5*		FR	(A1)	132-132
	0 No credit	*Booklet 2*		*Q23*	
	1 Partial Credit	*Booklet 3*		*Q11*	
	2 Full Credit	*Booklet 7*		*Q44*	
	3 Full Credit				
	9 Missing				
	n N/A				
	r Not reached				
R119Q06	*Gift – Q6*		MC	(A1)	133-133
	1 No Credit	*Booklet 2*		*Q20*	
	2 Full Credit	*Booklet 3*		*Q8*	
	3 No Credit	*Booklet 7*		*Q41*	
	4 No Credit				
	8 M/R				
	9 Missing				
	n N/A				
	r Not reached				
R119Q07	*Gift – Q7*		FR	(A1)	134-134
	0 No credit	*Booklet 2*		*19*	
	1 Partial Credit	*Booklet 3*		*Q7*	
	2 Partial Credit	*Booklet 7*		*Q40*	
	3 Full Credit				
	9 Missing				
	n N/A				
	r Not reached				
R119Q08	*Gift – Q8*		FR	(A1)	135-135
	0 No credit	*Booklet 2*		*Q21*	
	1 Full Credit	*Booklet 3*		*Q9*	
	2 Full Credit	*Booklet 7*		*Q42*	
	9 Missing				
	n N/A				
	r Not reached				
R119Q09T	*Gift – Q9*		FR	(A1)	136-136
	0 No credit	*Booklet 2*		*Q17*	
	1 Partial Credit	*Booklet 3*		*Q5*	
	2 Full Credit	*Booklet 7*		*Q38*	
	9 Missing				
	n N/A				
	r Not reached				

R120Q01	*Opinions – Q1*		MC	(A1)	137-137
	1 No Credit	*Booklet 4*		Q41	
	2 Full Credit	*Booklet 6*		Q25	
	3 No Credit	*Booklet 7*		Q8	
	4 No Credit				
	8 M/R				
	9 Missing				
	n N/A				
	r Not reached				
R120Q03	*Opinions – Q3*		MC	(A1)	138-138
	1 Full Credit	*Booklet 4*		Q42	
	2 No Credit	*Booklet 6*		Q26	
	3 No Credit	*Booklet 7*		Q9	
	4 No Credit				
	8 M/R				
	9 Missing				
	n N/A				
	r Not reached				
R120Q06	*Opinions – Q6*		FR	(A1)	139-139
	0 No credit	*Booklet 4*		Q43	
	1 Full Credit	*Booklet 6*		Q27	
	9 Missing	*Booklet 7*		Q10	
	n N/A				
	r Not reached				
R120Q07T	*Opinions – Q7*		CMC	(A1)	140-140
	0 No credit	*Booklet 4*		Q44	
	1 No credit	*Booklet 6*		Q28	
	2 No credit	*Booklet 7*		Q11	
	3 Full Credit				
	8 M/R				
	9 Missing				
	n N/A				
	r Not reached				
R122Q02	*Just Art – Q2*		MC	(A1)	141-141
	1 No Credit	*Booklet 2*		Q31	
	2 No Credit	*Booklet 4*		Q26	
	3 No Credit	*Booklet 5*		Q8	
	4 Full Credit				
	8 M/R				
	9 Missing				
	n N/A				
	r Not reached				

R122Q03T	*Just Art — Q3*		CMC	(A1)	142-142
	0 No credit	*Booklet 2*		*Q32*	
	1 No credit	*Booklet 4*		*Q27*	
	2 No credit	*Booklet 5*		*Q9*	
	3 No credit				
	4 No credit				
	5 Partial Credit				
	6 Full Credit				
	8 M/R				
	9 Missing				
	n N/A				
	r Not reached				
R216Q01	*Amanda — Q1*		MC	(A1)	143-143
	1 No Credit	*Booklet 8*		*Q52*	
	2 No Credit	*Booklet 9*		*Q39*	
	3 Full Credit				
	4 No Credit				
	8 M/R				
	9 Missing				
	n N/A				
	r Not reached				
R216Q02	*Amanda — Q2*		FR	(A1)	144-144
	0 No Credit	*Booklet 8*		*Q53*	
	1 Full credit	*Booklet 9*		*Q40*	
	9 Missing				
	n N/A				
	r Not reached				
R216Q03T	*Amanda — Q3*		FR	(A1)	145-145
	0 No credit	*Booklet 8*		*Q54*	
	1 Full Credit	*Booklet 9*		*Q41*	
	9 Missing				
	n N/A				
	r Not reached				
R216Q04	*Amanda — Q4*		FR	(A1)	146-146
	0 No credit	*Booklet 8*		*Q55*	
	1 Full Credit	*Booklet 9*		*Q42*	
	9 Missing				
	n N/A				
	r Not reached				

R216Q06	*Amanda – Q6*		MC	(A1)	147-147
	1 No Credit	*Booklet 8*		*Q56*	
	2 No Credit	*Booklet 9*		*Q43*	
	3 No Credit				
	4 Full Credit				
	8 M/R				
	9 Missing				
	n N/A				
	r Not reached				
R219Q01T	*Employment – Q1*		FR	(A1)	149-149
	0 No credit	*Booklet 0*		*Q1*	
	1 Full Credit	*Booklet 1*		*Q1*	
	9 Missing	*Booklet 5*		*Q33*	
	n N/A	*Booklet 7*		*Q17*	
	r Not reached				
R219Q01E	*Employment – Q1*		FR	(A1)	148-148
	0 No credit	*Booklet 0*		*Q1E*	
	1 Full Credit	*Booklet 1*		*Q1E*	
	9 Missing	*Booklet 5*		*Q33E*	
	n N/A	*Booklet 7*		*Q17E*	
	r Not reached				
R219Q02	*Employment – Q2*		FR	(A1)	150-150
	0 No credit	*Booklet 0*		*Q2*	
	1 Full Credit	*Booklet 1*		*Q2*	
	9 Missing	*Booklet 5*		*Q34*	
	n N/A	*Booklet 7*		*Q18*	
	r Not reached				
R220Q01	*South Pole – Q1*		FR	(A1)	151-151
	0 No credit	*Booklet 4*		*Q45*	
	1 Full Credit	*Booklet 6*		*Q29*	
	9 Missing	*Booklet 7*		*Q12*	
	n N/A				
	r Not reached				
R220Q02B	*South Pole – Q2*		MC	(A1)	152-152
	1 Full Credit	*Booklet 4*		*Q46*	
	2 No Credit	*Booklet 6*		*Q30*	
	3 No Credit	*Booklet 7*		*Q13*	
	4 No Credit				
	8 M/R				
	9 Missing				
	n N/A				
	r Not reached				

R220Q04	*South Pole – Q4*		MC	(A1)	153-153
	1 No Credit	*Booklet 4*		Q47	
	2 No Credit	*Booklet 6*		Q31	
	3 No Credit	*Booklet 7*		Q14	
	4 Full Credit				
	8 M/R				
	9 Missing				
	n N/A				
	r Not reached				
R220Q05	*South Pole – Q5*		MC	(A1)	154-154
	1 No Credit	*Booklet 4*		Q48	
	2 No Credit	*Booklet 6*		Q32	
	3 Full Credit	*Booklet 7*		Q15	
	4 No Credit				
	8 M/R				
	9 Missing				
	n N/A				
	r Not reached				
R220Q06	*South Pole – Q6*		MC	(A1)	155-155
	1 No Credit	*Booklet 4*		Q49	
	2 No Credit	*Booklet 6*		Q33	
	3 Full Credit	*Booklet 7*		Q16	
	4 No Credit				
	8 M/R				
	9 Missing				
	n N/A				
	r Not reached				
R225Q02	*Nuclear – Q2*		FR	(A1)	156-156
	0 No credit	*Booklet 0*		Q4	
	1 Full Credit	*Booklet 1*		Q21	
	9 Missing	*Booklet 2*		Q4	
	n N/A	*Booklet 6*		Q37	
	r Not reached				
R225Q03	*Nuclear – Q3*		MC	(A1)	157-157
	1 No Credit	*Booklet 0*		Q5	
	2 Full Credit	*Booklet 1*		Q22	
	3 No Credit	*Booklet 2*		Q5	
	4 No Credit	*Booklet 6*		Q38	
	8 M/R				
	9 Missing				
	n N/A				
	r Not reached				

R225Q04	*Nuclear – Q4*		MC	(A1)	158-158
	1 No Credit	*Booklet 0*		Q6	
	2 Full Credit	*Booklet 1*		Q23	
	3 No Credit	*Booklet 2*		Q6	
	4 No Credit	*Booklet 6*		Q39	
	8 M/R				
	9 Missing				
	n N/A				
	r Not reached				
R227Q01	*Optician – Q1*		MC	(A1)	159-159
	1 No Credit	*Booklet 1*		Q30	
	2 Full Credit	*Booklet 3*		Q12	
	3 No Credit	*Booklet 4*		Q1	
	4 No Credit				
	8 M/R				
	9 Missing				
	n N/A				
	r Not reached				
R227Q02T	*Optician – Q2*		CMC	(A1)	160-160
	0 No credit	*Booklet 1*		Q31	
	1 No credit	*Booklet 3*		Q13	
	2 No credit	*Booklet 4*		Q2	
	3 No credit				
	4 No credit				
	5 Partial Credit				
	6 Partial Credit				
	7 Full Credit				
	8 M/R				
	9 Missing				
	n N/A				
	r Not reached				
R227Q03	*Optician – Q3*		FR	(A1)	161-161
	0 No credit	*Booklet 1*		Q32	
	1 Full Credit	*Booklet 3*		Q14	
	9 Missing	*Booklet 4*		Q3	
	n N/A				
	r Not reached				
R227Q04	*Optician – Q4*		FR	(A1)	162-162
	0 No credit	*Booklet 1*		Q33	
	1 Partial Credit	*Booklet 3*		Q15	
	2 Full Credit	*Booklet 4*		Q4	
	9 Missing				
	n N/A				
	r Not reached				

R227Q06	*Optician — Q6*		FR	(A1)	163-163
	0 No credit	*Booklet 1*		*Q34*	
	1 Full Credit	*Booklet 3*		*Q16*	
	9 Missing	*Booklet 4*		*Q5*	
	n N/A				
	r Not reached				
R228Q01	*Guide — Q1*		MC	(A1)	164-164
	1 No Credit	*Booklet 4*		*Q34*	
	2 No Credit	*Booklet 6*		*Q18*	
	3 No Credit	*Booklet 7*		*Q1*	
	4 Full Credit				
	8 M/R				
	9 Missing				
	n N/A				
	r Not reached				
R228Q02	*Guide — Q2*		MC	(A1)	165-165
	1 No Credit	*Booklet 4*		*Q35*	
	2 Full Credit	*Booklet 6*		*Q19*	
	3 No Credit	*Booklet 7*		*Q2*	
	4 No Credit				
	8 M/R				
	9 Missing				
	n N/A				
	r Not reached				
R228Q04	*Guide — Q4*		MC	(A1)	166-166
	1 No Credit	*Booklet 4*		*Q36*	
	2 No Credit	*Booklet 6*		*Q20*	
	3 No Credit	*Booklet 7*		*Q3*	
	4 Full Credit				
	8 M/R				
	9 Missing				
	n N/A				
	r Not reached				
R234Q01	*Personnel — Q1*		FR	(A1)	167-167
	0 No credit	*Booklet 1*		*Q26*	
	1 Full Credit	*Booklet 2*		*Q9*	
	9 Missing	*Booklet 6*		*Q42*	
	n N/A				
	r Not reached				

R234Q02	*Personnel – Q2*		FR	(A1)	168-168
	0 No credit	*Booklet 1*		*Q27*	
	1 Full Credit	*Booklet 2*		*Q10*	
	9 Missing	*Booklet 6*		*Q43*	
	n N/A				
	r Not reached				
R236Q01	*NewRules – Q1*		FR	(A1)	169-169
	0 No credit	*Booklet 7*		*Q51*	
	1 Full Credit	*Booklet 8*		*Q41*	
	9 Missing	*Booklet 9*		*Q60*	
	n N/A				
	r Not reached				
R236Q02	*NewRules – Q2*		FR	(A1)	170-170
	0 No credit	*Booklet 7*		*Q52*	
	1 Full Credit	*Booklet 8*		*Q42*	
	2 Full Credit	*Booklet 9*		*Q61*	
	9 Missing				
	n N/A				
	r Not reached				
R237Q01	*Job Interview –*		FR	(A1)	171-171
	0 No credit	*Booklet 7*		*Q49*	
	1 Full Credit	*Booklet 8*		*Q39*	
	9 Missing	*Booklet 9*		*Q58*	
	n N/A				
	r Not reached				
R237Q03	*Job Interview –*		FR	(A1)	172-172
	0 No credit	*Booklet 7*		*Q50*	
	1 Full Credit	*Booklet 8*		*Q40*	
	9 Missing	*Booklet 9*		*Q59*	
	n N/A				
	r Not reached				
R238Q01	*Bicycle – Q1*		FR	(A1)	173-173
	0 No credit	*Booklet 1*		*Q24*	
	1 Full Credit	*Booklet 2*		*Q7*	
	9 Missing	*Booklet 6*		*Q40*	
	n N/A				
	r Not reached				
R238Q02	*Bicycle – Q2*		FR	(A1)	174-174
	0 No credit	*Booklet 1*		*Q25*	
	1 Full Credit	*Booklet 2*		*Q8*	
	9 Missing	*Booklet 6*		*Q41*	
	n N/A				
	r Not reached				

R239Q01	*Allergies – Q1*		FR	(A1)	175-175
	0 No credit	*Booklet 7*		*Q55*	
	1 Full Credit	*Booklet 8*		*Q45*	
	9 Missing	*Booklet 9*		*Q64*	
	n N/A				
	r Not reached				

R239Q02	*Allergies – Q2*		FR	(A1)	176-176
	0 No credit	*Booklet 7*		*Q56*	
	1 Full Credit	*Booklet 8*		*Q46*	
	9 Missing	*Booklet 9*		*Q65*	
	n N/A				
	r Not reached				

R241Q02	*WarrantyHotPoin*		FR	(A1)	177-177
	0 No credit	*Booklet 1*		*Q29*	
	1 Full Credit	*Booklet 2*		*Q12*	
	9 Missing	*Booklet 6*		*Q45*	
	n N/A				
	r Not reached				

R245Q01	*MovieReviews – Q1*		FR	(A1)	178-178
	0 No credit	*Booklet 1*		*Q18*	
	1 Full Credit	*Booklet 2*		*Q1*	
	9 Missing	*Booklet 6*		*Q34*	
	n N/A				
	r Not reached				

R245Q02	*MovieReviews – Q2*		FR	(A1)	179-179
	0 No credit	*Booklet 1*		*Q19*	
	1 Full Credit	*Booklet 2*		*Q2*	
	9 Missing	*Booklet 6*		*Q35*	
	n N/A				
	r Not reached				

R246Q01	*Contact Employe*		FR	(A1)	180-180
	0 No credit	*Booklet 7*		*Q53*	
	1 Full Credit	*Booklet 8*		*Q43*	
	9 Missing	*Booklet 9*		*Q62*	
	n N/A				
	r Not reached				

R246Q02	*Contact Employe*		FR	(A1)	181-181
	0 No credit	*Booklet 7*		*Q54*	
	1 Full Credit	*Booklet 8*		*Q44*	
	9 Missing	*Booklet 9*		*Q63*	
	n N/A				
	r Not reached				

S114Q03T	*Greenhouse – Q3*		FR	(A1)	182-182
	0 No credit	*Booklet 2*		Q43
	1 Full Credit	*Booklet 8*		Q21
	9 Missing			
	n N/A			
	r Not reached			
S114Q04T	*Greenhouse – Q4*		FR	(A1)	183-183
	0 No credit	*Booklet 2*		Q44
	1 Partial Credit	*Booklet 8*	Q22	
	2 Full Credit			
	9 Missing			
	n N/A			
	r Not reached			
S114Q05T	*Greenhouse – Q5*		FR	(A1)	184-184
	0 No credit	*Booklet 2*		Q45
	1 Full Credit	*Booklet 8*		Q23
	9 Missing			
	n N/A			
	r Not reached			
S128Q01	*Cloning – Q1*		MC	(A1)	185-185
	1 Full Credit	*Booklet 0*		Q25
	2 No Credit	*Booklet 2*		Q51
	3 No Credit	*Booklet 6*		Q49
	4 No Credit	*Booklet 9*		Q13
	8 M/R			
	9 Missing			
	n N/A			
	r Not reached			
S128Q02	*Cloning – Q2*		MC	(A1)	186-186
	1 Full Credit	*Booklet 2*		Q52
	2 No Credit	*Booklet 6*		Q50
	3 No Credit	*Booklet 9*		Q14
	4 No Credit			
	8 M/R			
	9 Missing			
	n N/A			
	r Not reached			
S128Q03T	*Cloning – Q3*		CMC	(A1)	187-187
	0 No credit	*Booklet 0*		Q26
	1 No credit	*Booklet 2*		Q53
	2 Full Credit	*Booklet 6*		Q51
	8 M/R			
	9 Missing			
	n N/A	*Booklet 9*		Q15
	r Not reached			

S129Q01	*Daylight – Q1*		MC	(A1)	188-188
	1 Full Credit	*Booklet 4*		*Q63*	
	2 No Credit	*Booklet 9*		*Q5*	
	3 No Credit				
	4 No Credit				
	8 M/R				
	9 Missing				
	n N/A				
	r Not reached				
S129Q02T	*Daylight – Q2*		FR	(A1)	189-189
	0 No credit	*Booklet 4*		*Q64*	
	1 Partial Credit	*Booklet 9*		*Q6*	
	2 Full Credit				
	9 Missing				
	n N/A				
	r Not reached				
S131Q02T	*GoodVibrations*		FR	(A1)	190-190
	0 No credit	*Booklet 2*		*Q54*	
	1 Full Credit	*Booklet 6*		*Q52*	
	9 Missing	*Booklet 9*		*Q16*	
	n N/A				
	r Not reached				
S131Q04T	*GoodVibrations*		FR	(A1)	191-191
	0 No credit	*Booklet 2*		*Q55*	
	1 Full Credit	*Booklet 6*		*Q53*	
	9 Missing	*Booklet 9*		*Q17*	
	n N/A				
	r Not reached				
S133Q01	*Research – Q1*		MC	(A1)	192-192
	1 No Credit	*Booklet 0*		*Q23*	
	2 No Credit	*Booklet 2*		*Q39*	
	3 Full Credit	*Booklet 8*		*Q17*	
	4 No Credit				
	8 M/R				
	9 Missing				
	n N/A				
	r Not reached				

S133Q03	Research — Q3		MC	(A1)	193-193
	1 Full Credit	Booklet 0		Q24	
	2 No Credit	Booklet 2		Q40	
	3 No Credit	Booklet 8		Q18	
	4 No Credit				
	8 M/R				
	9 Missing				
	n N/A				
	r Not reached				
S133Q04T	Research — Q4		CMC	(A1)	194-194
	0 No credit	Booklet 2		Q41	
	1 No credit	Booklet 8		Q19	
	2 No credit				
	3 Full Credit				
	8 M/R				
	9 Missing				
	n N/A				
	r Not reached				
S195Q02T	Semmelweis — Q2		FR	(A1)	195-195
	0 No credit	Booklet 4		Q50	
	1 Partial Credit	Booklet 6		Q54	
	2 Full Credit	Booklet 8		Q26	
	9 Missing				
	n N/A				
	r Not reached				
S195Q04	Semmelweis — Q4		MC	(A1)	196-196
	1 Full Credit	Booklet 4		Q51	
	2 No Credit	Booklet 6		Q55	
	3 No Credit	Booklet 8		Q27	
	4 No Credit				
	8 M/R				
	9 Missing				
	n N/A				
	r Not reached				
S195Q05T	Semmelweis — Q5		FR	(A1)	197-197
	0 No credit	Booklet 0		Q29	
	1 Full Credit	Booklet 4		Q52	
	9 Missing	Booklet 6		Q56	
	n N/A	Booklet 8		Q28	
	r Not reached				

S195Q06	*SemmelWeis – Q6*		MC	(A1)	198-198
	1 No Credit	*Booklet 0*		*Q30*	
	2 Full Credit	*Booklet 4*		*Q53*	
	3 No Credit	*Booklet 6*		*Q57*	
	4 No Credit	*Booklet 8*		*Q29*	
	8 M/R				
	9 Missing				
	n N/A				
	r Not reached				
S209Q02T	*Tidal Power – Q2*		FR	(A1)	199-199
	0 No credit	*Booklet 4*		*Q58*	
	1 Full Credit	*Booklet 6*		*Q62*	
	9 Missing	*Booklet 8*		*Q34*	
	n N/A				
	r Not reached				
S213Q01T	*Clothes – Q1*		CMC	(A1)	200-200
	0 No credit	*Booklet 2*		*Q46*	
	1 No credit	*Booklet 8*		*Q24*	
	2 No credit				
	3 No credit				
	4 Full Credit				
	8 M/R				
	9 Missing				
	n N/A				
	r Not reached				
S213Q02	*Clothes – Q2*		MC	(A1)	201-201
	1 Full Credit	*Booklet 2*		*Q47*	
	2 No Credit	*Booklet 8*		*Q25*	
	3 No Credit				
	4 No Credit				
	8 M/R				
	9 Missing				
	n N/A				
	r Not reached				
S252Q01	*SouthRainea – Q1*		MC	(A1)	202-202
	1 No Credit	*Booklet 0*		*Q27*	
	2 No Credit	*Booklet 4*		*Q54*	
	3 Full Credit	*Booklet 6*		*Q58*	
	4 No Credit	*Booklet 8*		*Q30*	
	8 M/R				
	9 Missing				
	n N/A				
	r Not reached				

S252Q02	SouthRainea – Q2		MC	(A1)	203-203
	1 Full Credit	Booklet 0		Q28	
	2 No Credit	Booklet 4		Q55	
	3 No Credit	Booklet 6		Q59	
	4 No Credit	Booklet 8		Q31	
	8 M/R				
	9 Missing				
	n N/A				
	r Not reached				

S252Q03T	SouthRainea – Q3		CMC	(A1)	204-204
	0 No credit	Booklet 4		Q56	
	1 No credit	Booklet 6		Q60	
	2 Full Credit	Booklet 8		Q32	
	8 M/R				
	9 Missing				
	n N/A				
	r Not reached				

S253Q01T	Ozone – Q1		FR	(A1)	205-205
	0 No credit	Booklet 4		Q59	
	1 Partial Credit	Booklet 9		Q1	
	2 Full Credit				
	3 Full Credit				
	9 Missing				
	n N/A				
	r Not reached				

S253Q02	Ozone – Q2		MC	(A1)	206-206
	1 No Credit	Booklet 4		Q60	
	2 Full Credit	Booklet 9		Q2	
	3 No Credit				
	4 No Credit				
	8 M/R				
	9 Missing				
	n N/A				
	r Not reached				

S253Q05	Ozone – Q5		FR	(A1)	207-207
	0 No credit	Booklet 4		Q61	
	1 Full Credit	Booklet 9		Q3	
	9 Missing				
	n N/A				
	r Not reached				

S256Q01	*Spoons — Q1*		MC	(A1)	208-208
	1 Full Credit	*Booklet 0*		Q21	
	2 No Credit	*Booklet 2*		Q42	
	3 No Credit	*Booklet 8*		Q20	
	4 No Credit				
	8 M/R				
	9 Missing				
	n N/A				
	r Not reached				

S268Q01	*Algae — Q1*		MC	(A1)	209-209
	1 No Credit	*Booklet 4*		Q65	
	2 No Credit	*Booklet 9*		Q7	
	3 Full Credit				
	4 No Credit				
	8 M/R				
	9 Missing				
	n N/A				
	r Not reached				

S268Q02T	*Algae — Q2*		FR	(A1)	210-210
	0 No credit	*Booklet 4*		Q66	
	1 Full Credit	*Booklet 9*		Q8	
	9 Missing				
	n N/A				
	r Not reached				

S268Q06	*Algae — Q6*		MC	(A1)	211-211
	1 No Credit	*Booklet 4*		Q67	
	2 Full Credit	*Booklet 9*		Q9	
	3 No Credit				
	4 No Credit				
	8 M/R				
	9 Missing				
	n N/A				
	r Not reached				

S269Q01	*Earth — Q1*		FR	(A1)	212-212
	0 No credit	*Booklet 0*		Q22	
	1 Full Credit	*Booklet 2*		Q48	
	9 Missing	*Booklet 6*		Q46	
	n N/A	*Booklet 9*		Q10	
	r Not reached				

S269Q03T	*Earth – Q3*		FR	(A1)	213-213
	0 No credit	*Booklet 2*		*Q49*	
	1 Full Credit	*Booklet 6*		*Q47*	
	9 Missing	*Booklet 9*		*Q11*	
	n N/A				
	r Not reached				
S269Q04T	*Earth – Q4*		CMC	(A1)	214-214
	0 No credit	*Booklet 2*		*Q50*	
	1 No credit	*Booklet 6*		*Q48*	
	2 No credit	*Booklet 9*		*Q12*	
	3 No credit				
	4 Full Credit				
	8 M/R				
	9 Missing				
	n N/A				
	r Not reached				
S270Q03T	*Ozone – Q3*		CMC	(A1)	215-215
	0 No credit	*Booklet 4*		*Q62*	
	1 No credit	*Booklet 9*		*Q4*	
	2 Full Credit				
	8 M/R				
	9 Missing				
	n N/A				
	r Not reached				
MSCALE	*Maths Scalable*			(A1)	217-217
RSCALE	*Reading Scalable*			(A1)	218-218
SSCALE	*Science Scalable*			(A1)	219-219
CLCUSE	*Calculator Use*			(A1)	221-221
	1 No calculator				
	2 A simple calculator				
	3 A scientific calculator				
	4 A programmable calculator				
	5 A graphics calculator				
	8 M/R				
	9 Mis				
	n N/A				
CNT	*Country alphanumeric code*			(A3)	223-225

APPENDIX 8 **SCORES ALLOCATED TO THE ITEMS**

	Score 1	Score 2	Score 3
M033Q01	4		
M034Q01T	1		
M037Q01T	1		
M037Q02T	1		
M124Q01	2		
M124Q03T	1	2	3
M136Q01T	2		
M136Q02T	1		
M136Q03T	1	2	
M144Q01T	1		
M144Q02T	1		
M144Q03	1		
M144Q04T	1		
M145Q01T	1		
M148Q02T	1	2	
M150Q01	1		
M150Q02T	1	2	
M150Q03T	1		
M155Q01	1		
M155Q02T	1	2	
M155Q03T	1	2	
M155Q04T	4		
M159Q01	2		
M159Q02	3		
M159Q03	2		
M159Q05	2		
M161Q01	4		
M179Q01T	1	2	
M192Q01T	2,3		
M266Q01T	4		
M273Q01T	1		

	Score 1	Score 2	Score 3
S114Q03T	1		
S114Q04T	1	2	
S114Q05T	1		
S128Q01	1		
S128Q02	1		
S128Q03T	2		
S129Q01	1		
S129Q02T	1	2	
S131Q02T	1		
S131Q04T	1		
S133Q01	3		
S133Q03	1		
S133Q04T	3		
S195Q02T	1	2	
S195Q04	1		
S195Q05T	1		
S195Q06	2		
S209Q02T	1		
S213Q01T	4		
S213Q02	1		
S252Q01	3		
S252Q02	1		
S252Q03T	2		
S253Q01T	1	2,3	
S253Q02	2		
S253Q05	1		
S256Q01	1		
S268Q01	3		
S268Q02T	1		
S268Q06	2		
S269Q01	1		
S269Q03T	1		
S269Q04T	4		
S270Q03T	2		

	Score 1	Score 2	Score 3	Reading Sub-scale
R040Q02	1			Retrieving information
R040Q03A	1			Retrieving information
R040Q03B	1			Reflecting
R040Q04	1			Interpreting
R040Q06	3			Interpreting
R055Q01	4			Interpreting
R055Q02	1			Reflecting
R055Q03	2			Interpreting
R055Q05	1			Interpreting
R061Q01	1,2			Interpreting
R061Q03	3			Interpreting
R061Q04	3			Interpreting
R061Q05	1			Reflecting
R067Q01	3			Interpreting
R067Q04	1	2		Reflecting
R067Q05	1	2		Reflecting
R070Q02	1			Retrieving information
R070Q03	3			Retrieving information
R070Q04	1			Reflecting
R070Q07T	4	5		Interpreting
R076Q03	1			Retrieving information
R076Q04	1			Interpreting
R076Q05	1			Retrieving information
R077Q02	2			Retrieving information
R077Q03	1	2		Reflecting
R077Q04	2			Interpreting
R077Q05	2			Reflecting
R077Q06	4			Interpreting
R081Q01	2			Interpreting
R081Q05	1			Interpreting
R081Q06A	1			Reflecting
R081Q06B	1			Reflecting
R083Q01	4			Interpreting
R083Q02	1			Retrieving information
R083Q03	1			Retrieving information

	Score 1	Score 2	Score 3	Reading Sub-scale
R083Q04	1			Interpreting
R083Q06	1			Reflecting
R086Q04	1			Reflecting
R086Q05	3			Interpreting
R086Q07	1			Reflecting
R088Q01	4			Interpreting
R088Q03	1	2		Retrieving information
R088Q04T	3,4	5		Interpreting
R088Q05T	3			Reflecting
R088Q07	3			Reflecting
R091Q05	1			Retrieving information
R091Q06	2			Interpreting
R091Q07B	2			Reflecting
R093Q03	1			Interpreting
R099Q04B	2	3		Reflecting
R100Q04	2			Retrieving information
R100Q05	3			Interpreting
R100Q06	3			Interpreting
R100Q07	2			Interpreting
R101Q01	3			Interpreting
R101Q02	2			Interpreting
R101Q03	2			Reflecting
R101Q04	3			Interpreting
R101Q05	4			Interpreting
R101Q08	3			Interpreting
R102Q01	2			Interpreting
R102Q04A	1			Interpreting
R102Q05	1			Interpreting
R102Q06	1			Reflecting
R102Q07	3			Interpreting
R104Q01	1			Retrieving information
R104Q02	1			Retrieving information
R104Q05	1	2		Retrieving information
R104Q06	1			Retrieving information
R110Q01	4			Interpreting

	Score 1	Score 2	Score 3	Reading Sub-scale
R110Q04	1			Retrieving information
R110Q05	1			Retrieving information
R110Q06	4			Reflecting
R111Q01	4			Interpreting
R111Q02B	1	2		Reflecting
R111Q04	3			Retrieving information
R111Q06B	1	2		Reflecting
R119Q01	3			Interpreting
R119Q04	3			Interpreting
R119Q05	1	2,3		Reflecting
R119Q06	2			Retrieving information
R119Q07	1,2	3		Interpreting
R119Q08	1,2			Interpreting
R119Q09T	1	2		Reflecting
R120Q01	2			Interpreting
R120Q03	1			Interpreting
R120Q06	1			Reflecting
R120Q07T	3			Reflecting
R122Q02	4			Interpreting
R122Q03T	5	6		Retrieving information
R216Q01	3			Interpreting
R216Q02	1			Reflecting
R216Q03T	1			Interpreting
R216Q04	1			Retrieving information
R216Q06	4			Interpreting
R219Q01T	1			Retrieving information
R219Q01E	1			Interpreting
R219Q02	1			Reflecting
R220Q01	1			Retrieving information
R220Q02B	1			Interpreting
R220Q04	4			Interpreting
R220Q05	3			Interpreting
R220Q06	3			Interpreting
R225Q02	1			Interpreting
R225Q03	2			Retrieving information

	Score 1	*Score 2*	*Score 3*	*Reading Sub-scale*
R225Q04	2			Retrieving information
R227Q01	2			Interpreting
R227Q02T	5,6	7		Retrieving information
R227Q03	1			Reflecting
R227Q04	1	2		Interpreting
R227Q06	1			Retrieving information
R228Q01	4			Interpreting
R228Q02	2			Interpreting
R228Q04	4			Interpreting
R234Q01	1			Retrieving information
R234Q02	1			Retrieving information
R236Q01	1			Interpreting
R236Q02	1,2			Interpreting
R237Q01	1			Retrieving information
R237Q03	1			Interpreting
R238Q01	1			Retrieving information
R238Q02	1			Interpreting
R239Q01	1			Interpreting
R239Q02	1			Retrieving information
R241Q02	1			Interpreting
R245Q01	1			Retrieving information
R245Q02	1			Interpreting
R246Q01	1			Retrieving information
R246Q02	1			Retrieving information

OECD PUBLICATIONS, 2, rue André-Pascal, 75775 PARIS CEDEX 16
PRINTED IN FRANCE
(96 2002 02 1 P) ISBN 92-64-19822-9 − No. 52583 2002